WITHDRAWN BY THE
UNIVERSITY OF MICHIGAN

Transportation, Temporal, and Spatial Components of Accessibility

Transportation, Temporal, and Spatial Components of Accessibility

Lawrence D. Burns
General Motors
Research Laboratories

LexingtonBooks
D.C. Heath and Company
Lexington, Massachusetts
Toronto

Transportation
Library

HE
336
.C5
B96

Library of Congress Cataloging in Publication Data

Burns, Lawrence D
  Transportation, temporal, and spatial components of accessibility.

  Bibliography: p.
  Includes index.
    1. Choice of transportation.   2.   Transportation—Mathematical
models.   3.   Space and time.   I.   Title.
HE336.C5B87   380'.5'1   79–1725
  ISBN 0–669–02916–5

Copyright © 1979 by D.C. Heath and Company.

All rights reserved. No part of this publication may be reproduced or trans-
mitted in any form or by any means, electronic or mechanical, including pho-
tocopy, recording, or any information storage or retrieval system, without
permission in writing from the publisher.

Published simultaneously in Canada.

Printed in the United States of America.

International Standard Book Number: 0–669–02916–5

Library of Congress Catalog Card Number: 79–1725

136147-236

*To my parents
and
in memory of Lauren Jay Burns*

Contents

List of Figures

List of Tables

Acknowledgments

The research contained in this book was completed while I was affiliated with the Civil Engineering Department and the Institute of Transportation Studies at the University of California, Berkeley. The arrangements for publishing this book were completed while I was affiliated with the Transportation and Traffic Science Department of the General Motors Research Laboratories.

A number of individuals contributed their time, expertise, support, and friendship in the preparation of this book. I would like to express my sincere appreciation to all of them. I would like to give special recognition to William L. Garrison, professor of civil engineering and director of the Institute of Transportation Studies, University of California, Berkeley. Professor Garrison provided invaluable encouragement and criticism of this book. In addition, Allan R. Pred, professor of geography, University of California, Berkeley, Pravin Varaiya, professor of electrical engineering and economics, University of California, Berkeley, and David Jones, research associate, Institute of Transportation Studies, University of California, Berkeley provided numerous insightful and useful comments.

I am also grateful for the opportunity provided to me by the Transportation and Traffic Science Department of the General Motors Research Laboratories to arrange to publish this book. William M. Spreitzer heads this department.

I would also like to thank Abraham D. Horowitz, Bruce A. Phillips, and Roger L. Tobin, all of the Transportation and Traffic Science Department of the General Motors Research Laboratories, and Professor Martin Wachs, of the School of Architecture and Urban Planning at the University of California, Los Angeles, for their numerous insightful comments.

Jan Roberts, Ruth Suziki, and Darlene Dragonajtys all typed portions of this book. Their patience and promptness are deeply appreciated. Fred Clarke, Jr. edited portions of the initial draft. His comments were very helpful.

Finally, and most important, I would like to thank my parents, brother, two sisters, and my very special friend Vera Nazione. Without their love, patience, and unquestioning support, this book would never have been a reality.

This project was funded in part by U.S. Department of Transportation contract No. DOT-OS-50237, "Managing the Future Evolution of the Urban Transportation System."

1 Introduction

Object of the Book

Accessibility is a concept used in a number of fields (for example, transportation planning, marketing, geography, and urban planning).[1] It has taken on a variety of meanings, including the physical proximity of two or more locations, the activity opportunities available in a geographical region, and the freedom of individuals to decide whether or not to participate in different activities (for example, work, shopping, and recreation). This study is concerned with accessibility in the latter context, that is, the freedom of individuals. As such, it focuses attention on constraints which limit this freedom and courses of action that can be taken to relax these constraints. These courses of action are called *strategies*.

Individuals face a wide variety of constraints that limit their accessibility. Some of these constraints take the form of economic, physiological, or psychological barriers. Others result from barriers imposed on individuals by their environment. Of interest here are constraints that exist because

Individuals can be at only one location at any given time.

Different activities are not available at all times and at all locations (that is, the availability of activities is unevenly distributed in time and in space).

Individuals can travel between locations only so fast, and therefore, their movements use time (that is, the transportation available to individuals does not allow them to move instantaneously).

Constraints that exist for these reasons are encompassed in what is regarded here to be the transportation, temporal, and spatial components of accessibility. Specifically, the *transportation component* of accessibility involves the transportation available to individuals and the speed at which this transportation allows individuals to overcome space. The *temporal component* involves the availability of activities at different times of the day and the times in which individuals participate in specific activities. And the *spatial component* involves the availability of activities in geographical space and the locations of specific activities that individuals participate in. Because travel consumes time and individuals can be at only one location at any given time, the temporal and spatial components of accessibility are interdependent.

1

The object of this book is to provide a methodological study of accessibility. By *methodological* it is meant that the study not only supplies a method of inquiry into the concept of accessibility, but also explores the logic of this method. Attention is focused on principles concerning the dependence of accessibility on its transportation, temporal, and spatial components, and on the accessibility implications of strategies affecting these components.

Traditions from which this Study Emerges

Accessibility, as it is conceptualized here, is a product of a broadly conceived urban activity system. This system encompasses the possible and actual ways in which individuals, households, institutions, and firms pursue their daily affairs in metropolitan communities and interact with one another in time and space.[2] Clearly, the possible and actual webs of relations between these entities are very complex. As a result, efforts to delve into the urban activity system are extremely ambitious undertakings.

There are numerous facets of the urban activity system that make for more or less accessibility. First and foremost, as far as this study is concerned, are the transportation available to individuals, the temporal and spatial distributions of activities, and the social and economic roles of individuals that determine when, where, and for how long they must pursue different activities. Recall that these facets encompass what are defined here to be the transportation, temporal, and spatial components of accessibility.

While not focused on directly here, differentials in income and wealth, sociopsychological capabilities, and political participation are also significant. Income and wealth influence purchasing power and hence power to choose. They bear on where one lives, what one can afford to do, what travel modes are at one's disposal, and how self–reliant one can be. Sociopsychological capabilities determine the knowledge, self–confidence, capacity for initiative, and other requisites for the effective searching out and use of possible opportunities. In addition, political participation determines one's ability to gain access to political power or influence and, therefore, one's ability to bring about change.

In light of the different facets of urban activity systems that affect accessibility, one recognizes that there are a number of courses of action or strategies that can serve to enhance accessibility. These strategies include improvements in transportation systems, removal or relaxation of temporal barriers, changes in the spatial distribution of activities, redistribution of income, more education concerning local environment, and facilitation of community participation in the political arena.

There is a rich tradition of studies of accessibility that are broadly conceived in the context of the urban activity system and that are strategic in nature (that is, they suggest responses to deal with the problem of accessibility). Included for exemplary purposes are the works of Owen[3], Chapin[4], Foley[5], and Hägerstrand[6].

Owen argues for considering urban areas as complex interacting systems. This comprehensive view suggests that temporal patterns of urban life and the geometries of spatial organization are critical ingredients in the performance of the urban transportation system in particular and the urban activity system in general. Strategies of response emerging from Owen's holistic view tend toward responses in the urban design tradition: joint planning of transportation and land use, growth management, and redevelopment.

Chapin, Foley, and Hägerstrand take a more microscopic view of the urban activity system. Chapin is concerned with the what and why of activity patterns as opposed to the where and why of location patterns. In short, he provides an understanding of the diversity of living patterns to be found in a city, with the idea of subsequently bringing this knowledge to bear in investment decisions. While Chapin's work focuses directly on explaining behavior, he recognizes that behavior depends to a great extent on the constraints individuals confront. As such, in addition to being deeply embedded in the tradition of the urban activity system, Chapin's work tangentially concerns the components of accessibility. It is strategic not in the sense of suggesting specific strategies, but in recognizing the existence of different "publics" who are affected by investment strategies in a variety of ways.

Like Chapin, Foley recognizes the uneven distribution of accessibility over the population and the dependence of accessibility on the urban activity system. Foley stresses the deprivation and nonaccess suffered by selected categories of residents in the midst of the larger trend toward affluence and access in the United States. He argues that the ubiquity of the automobile has led analysts and decisionmakers to think that most Americans are well served by the automobile and that this has permitted urban land-use patterns and transportation systems to cater primarily to automobile users. This has been to the specific and serious deprivation of those who lack access to the automobile. Foley suggests that the public-policy implications of this situation involve the need for improving the accessibility of those people who have failed to fully share the benefits of residence in metropolitan environs. From a strategic standpoint, he argues that undue emphasis has probably been placed in recent years on the promise of improved transportation. As an alternative, he suggests focusing on improved access to shifting job opportunities, income maintenance, and the physical health of the populace. He also argues for the thoughtful provision of selected local opportunities and innovative types of service centers in local residential districts which specialize in providing information about the larger webs of essentially nonlocal facilities. Like Owen, Foley's suggested strategies have a spatial flavor.

Finally, Hägerstrand emphasizes that the prediction of urban form or the creation of urban form through physical planning will remain only superficially successful until a better understanding is gained of how urban form and human behavior are related. Like Owen, Chapin, and Foley, Hägerstrand has a very broad conception of the urban activity system and the dependence of human behavior on the complex webs formed by the components of this system.

Hägerstrand argues that the analyst should give up efforts to predict behavior directly and, instead, focus attention on finding out how limits to freedom of action come about. As such, Hägerstrand is directly concerned with accessibility. His work in this area provides the foundation around which the present study of accessibility is structured.

Hägerstrand's work, like the present study, is strategic in a very broad sense. Not only does it suggest the pursuit of more conventional urban design and transportation planning strategies, but it also suggests the consideration of a variety of nonconventional strategies, such as the introduction of flexible work hours, company-sponsored van pools, extended hours for public services, and the joint planning and coordinating of shopping centers, industrial parks, and child-care facilities.

While the studies of accessibility mentioned here are broadly conceptualized in terms of the urban activity system and rich from a strategic standpoint, they do not provide robust analytical tools for the systematic evaluation and comparison of different strategies. This book, thoroughly grounded in the tradition of these earlier studies, provides such an analytical treatment.

Motivation

The accessibility of individuals and the effects of different strategies on this accessibility is of interest for a number of practicable reasons. First, implicit in the concern for the freedom of individuals is the view that public policy should include a concern for providing individuals with a greater ability to realize their desires. That is, public policy should provide individuals a greater set of options to choose from, and it should distribute these options among the population in more equitable ways. Viewing public policy as an "enabling ethic" places one directly in line with such traditional values as individualism, personal freedom, and the right to access to public goods.

Because of the historical roots and strengths of these values in many societies, knowledge of where the limits to individual freedom come from and the effects of different strategies on these limits is paramount.

Second, there is strong evidence that suggests that individuals value accessibility. This evidence includes the migration of individuals to opportunity-rich cities and the ubiquity of accessibility-enhancing innovations such as the automobile and the telephone. Because of the importance of accessibility to individuals, an understanding of the determinants of accessibility, as well as of the relative advantages of different strategies that enhance accessibility, is of further importance.

Third, a number of problems are currently emerging which threaten to reduce the accessibility of individuals. Included are the energy issue, inflation, the fiscal austerity of cities, and the restrictive housing investment market. Insights into the manner in which these problems may limit the freedom of individuals are necessary to an evaluation of the impacts of such problems. Through a methodological study of accessibility, such insights may ultimately be provided and strategies serving to counteract these potential accessibility losses may surface.

Finally, accessibility-deprived individuals in American society are gaining an increasingly strong voice. In fact, the rights of the physical and mentally handicapped, the poor, the elderly, children, minorities, and women are collectively receiving more attention today than they have at any point in our history. To guarantee the rights of such individuals, it is necessary to have an understanding of how the accessibility of these individuals is limited and how these limits can be relaxed.

Approach

In focusing on accessibility, this study does not attempt to predict changes in individual or societal behavior which result from alternative strategies. Instead, attention is focused on the impacts of strategies on behavioral constraints which, in both obvious and subtle ways, limit the freedom of individuals to participate in different activities and therefore limit their accessibility.

This emphasis on behavioral constraints has two rationales. First, since what individuals are free to do—as well as what they actually do—is important, the accessibility implications of different strategies should be evaluated. This is especially true when the distribution of impacts is considered. Second, much can be learned about individual and societal behavior by analyzing conditions which circumscribe behavior. One cannot be certain which aspects of behavior result from constraining circumstances and which express individual preferences as they would be revealed freely if the constraints were relaxed.[7]

Underlying this study of accessibility is a space–time representation of human activity developed by Torsten Hägerstrand for his time–geography model of society.[8] This representation simultaneously considers factors which limit freedom of action over time and in space. Its forte is its ability to systematically and diagrammatically reveal the spatial and temporal characteristics of behavioral constraints and the spatial and temporal implications of strategies influencing these constraints.

An introduction to Hägerstrand's framework is provided in chapter 2. This framework is then applied in chapter 3 to diagrammatically assess the accessibility implications of various transportation, temporal, and spatial strategies.

To analyze and compare the implications of different strategies, accessibility measures are needed. Chapter 4 provides a generalized approach to measuring accessibility. This measurement framework allows the formation of a variety of analytical measures based on different perspectives on individuals' valuations of their space–time opportunities, and on a wide range of idealized conditions (such as idealized network geometries and activity distributions). Chapter 5 develops and applies such measures in a number of simple cases. Principles result from these simple cases which are applicable when evaluating strategies with respect to complex real–world conditions. These principles lead to general conclusions regarding the relative attractiveness of strategies conceived to enhance the accessibilities of individuals. As such, the general analytical approach provides a format which can be extended to aid in making decisions between policy alternatives and leads to the establishment of policy–relevant conclusions that are robust over a wide range of real–world conditions.

While the salient contributions of this book emerge from the analytical study of accessibility provided in chapters 4 and 5, empirics are not totally neglected. Specifically, chapter 6 supplements the analytical study by providing a variety of empirical insights. Initially, typical values of the variables incorporated in the accessibility measures developed here and insights into trends in these values are presented in chapter 6. Next, common observations regarding accessibility are assessed in the context of these data and insights, and in the context of the accessibility methodology. Finally, the data needed for a detailed empirical analysis of accessibility, how these data could be collected, and the questions to which they would be applied are discussed.

Because the conceptual framework developed here is quite broad, its applicability and the issues it raises cannot be exhausted in a single study. In light of this, a discussion of the need for and directions of future research in accessibility modeling is presented in chapter 7.

Scope

The accessibility methodology developed and analyzed here is viewed as a supplement to conventional urban transportation planning methodologies. These conventional methodologies were conceived during an era in which the urban transportation problem was defined primarily in terms of the problem of congestion. As such, traditional methods are predominantly oriented toward facilities planning. They emphasize matching supplies of transportation services with projected travel demands. Given that the era of facilities planning in transportation is winding down for now,[9] the relevance of methodologies developed to address the problem of congestion is waning and there is a preeminent need for fresh approaches to a broadening conceptualization of the transportation problem. While not a panacea, the present study of accessibility provides such an approach.

An advantage of the accessibility methodology is that it richly defines the role of personal transportation in the broad context of its enabling role. This is in contrast to conventional transportation planning methodologies, which tend to narrowly conceive of personal transportation as trip making or flows on networks and neglect factors that generate and condition these trips and flows. Specifically, the accessibility methodology recognizes that personal transportation enables individuals to reach locations of activities that are distributed in both space and time. While it is an essential component of accessibility, much more than transportation is involved in providing accessibility. As such, transportation strategies are only a subset of accessibility-enhancing strategies, and therefore, they must be evaluated relative to strategies that traditionally are not the concern of transportation planners. This confronts the logic of past approaches to the study of transportation which view transportation as a separate entity removed from the broader accessibility system of which it is a part. It also avoids the problem of overexploiting strategies of a single type (for example, transportation strategies) and therefore experiencing diminishing returns on efforts to enhance accessibility.

Viewing transportation in the context of its enabling function provides a conception of the benefits of personal transportation that differs from the conception of benefits underlying conventional evaluative methodologies. These conventional methodologies emphasize interdependencies between observed trip-making patterns and transportation-system/land-use characteristics. The classical measure of benefit underlying them is the value of the aggregate travel-time savings that result from different strategies developed to meet projected travel volumes. This criterion relies heavily on projections of future travel volumes and estimates of an average system user's value of time.

The quest for an alternative conception of the benefits of personal transportation is not intended to suggest that travel-time savings are not benefits. Rather, this quest emanates from a realization that travel-volume—travel-time criteria are quite narrow in light of the comprehensiveness of present-day transportation issues (for example, issues concerned with social equity, resource conservation, environmental quality, efficiency, and economic growth and stabilization). This narrowness stems primarily from the dependence of travel-volume—travel-time criteria on observed trip-making patterns. Granted, concern must be given to the externalities of travel that result from observed trips. Energy is not consumed, air is not polluted, and congestion does not result until trips are made. However, attempting to capture the underlying determinants of these trips and to simultaneously structure the nature of transportation benefits by concentrating solely on trips is insufficient in two important respects.

First, by directing policies toward matching supplies of transportation services with observed travel demands, differences in the transportation services provided to different groups of individuals are propagated. Along this same line, travel-time reductions are indicators of benefits accruing to individuals capable of using existing systems. Therefore, formulation of majoritarian welfare functions that express net benefits in terms of total travel-time savings results in biases toward policies which further perpetuate the mobility disadvantages of certain individuals.

Second, travel-volume—travel-time criteria focus the attention of policymakers and transportation agencies on the performance of transportation facilities. For this reason, the primary concern of these decision-makers is for the efficient provision of additional capacity to reduce existing and anticipated congestion and for the efficient use of existing facilities through the control and management of travel demand (that is, flows on networks). Factors that condition the ability of individuals to use transportation facilities and therefore the distribution of transportation services to various individuals are typically neglected.

The accessibility methodology provides a conception of the benefits of transportation in terms of the spatial and temporal autonomy of individuals rather than in terms of their actual trip-making behavior. Such an approach is predicated on the notion that what individuals are free to do as well as what they actually do is important.[10]

Viewing the benefits of transportation in the context of accessibility places the travel-time-savings benefit measure in a new light. Rather than placing monetary value on the travel-time savings resulting from different strategies, the accessibility methodology views these travel-time savings in the context of how the velocity increases that generated them enlarge the opportunity space of individuals. For this reason, importance is not placed on the amount of time that can be saved, but rather on the manner in which improved velocities enhance the freedom of individuals to partake in activities. In so doing, the accessibility methodology does not multiply travel-time savings for individuals into large social aggregates which are purported to represent the benefits of transportation facility improvements.

It is also important to note that the accessibility-measurement framework developed here as part of the accessibility methodology differs significantly from past efforts to measure accessibility. Most past studies view accessibility in the geographical sense of physical proximity between two locations or between a location of reference and a set of locations having varying levels of attraction. In these studies, accessibility is an attribute of locations and depends on the transportation facilities serving locations and the spatial distribution of activities relative to locations. The traditional concern for accessibility has therefore been concern for the performance of transportation facilities and for the locations of residences, firms, and a variety of service and recreational activities (for example, shopping centers, banks, hospitals, and parks). For this reason, most past measures of accessibility[11] have been developed either to evaluate the transportation services provided to different locations or to assess the locational advantages (or disadvantages) of different locations.

By viewing accessibility in the context of the freedom of individuals, the measurement framework developed here differs from previous approaches in four distinct ways. First, the present framework is developed relative to individuals as opposed to locations. Second, this framework encompasses both the spatial and temporal dimensions of accessibility in a manner that maintains their inseparability. This is in contrast to virtually all existing approaches to measuring accessibility which reflect only the spatial dimension. By incorporating the temporal dimension, the framework developed here integrates the conventional spatial tools (for example, gravity models and spatial-accessibility measures) and temporal tools (benefit measures based on travel-time savings) of transportation planners and engineers into a single framework that is applicable in systematically evaluating a broad variety of accessibility-enhancing strategies (that is, transportation, temporal, and spatial strategies).

Third, the framework views accessibility measures as *value-weighted mappings* of the opportunities comprising the behavioral spaces of individuals. As such, it highlights the fact that accessibility measures are subjective; that is, every measure of accessibility is based on assumptions regarding how individuals value the opportunities defined by their behavioral space. This points to the necessity of evaluating different accessibility-enhancing strategies using a variety of accessibility measures based on different perspectives regarding the way individuals value opportunities. Furthermore, it challenges the relevance of studies that draw conclusions regarding accessibility based on a single ad hoc measure.

The final unique characteristic of the accessibility-measurement framework developed here is its analytical flexibility. Rather than attempting to develop empirical measures of accessibility based on a unique set of real-world conditions, the framework concentrates on developing analytical measures of accessibility based on idealized assumptions concerning a wide range of real-world conditions. The rationale behind this is twofold.

First, it is felt that little is gained from taking a set of data and transforming it into a measure with accessibility units. Such an approach only provides information about the unique real-world circumstances corresponding to the data under consideration. Furthermore, final numbers which purport to be measures of accessibility may have little policy relevance.

Second, for purposes of policy analysis, the *marginal* effectiveness of different accessibility-enhancing strategies under different circumstances are of interest. Empirical measures are generally not conducive to such marginal analysis, while closed-form analytical measures are ideal. As such, the general analytical approach adopted here provides a format which can be extended to aid in choosing between policy alternatives and leads to the establishment of policy-relevant conclusions that are robust over a wide range of real-world conditions.

Table 1-1 summarizes the scope of this study by comparing it with conventional studies related to accessibility and urban transportation.

Table 1-1
Summary of the Scope of this Study

Item Treated	This Study Emphasizes	Past Studies Emphasized
Meaning of accessibility	Freedom of individuals to decide to participate in different activities	Physical proximity or geographical reach and density of transport links
Unit of analysis	Individuals (with the potential to aggregate to households)	Transportation facilities or geographical zones
Thrust of public policy	Allow individuals more freedom to participate in activities and/or distribute this freedom more equitably	Efficiently match supply of transportation facilities with demand; control and management of demand
Components of accessibility considered	Transportation, temporal, and spatial	Transportation and spatial
Modeling orientation	Descriptive	Predictive
Focus	Contraints on behavior	Observed behavior
Type of accessibility measures	Analytical	Empirical
View of personal transportation	A component of the accessibility system	A separate system
Strategies that are compared	Transportation, temporal, *and* spatial	Transportation only *or* spatial only

2 Hägerstrand's Space–Time Representation of Human Activity

A space–time representation of human activity developed by Hägerstrand[1] for his time–geography model of society provides the fundamental paradigm underlying the present study of accessibility.[2] In this paradigm, every action and event which in sequence compose an individual's existence are recognized to have both temporal and spatial attributes—not merely one or the other. As such, time and space are seen as inseparable. This inseparability is represented diagrammatically in figure 2–1. Here, geographical space is compressed into a two-dimensional surface, and time is represented along the vertical axis. Within this framework, an individual's existence is described as an unbroken trajectory through space and time. As long as an individual is stationary in space, his trajectory is moving parallel to the time axis. When an individual is moving in space, he is also moving in time, resulting in an inclined trajectory with the angle being a function of speed (low speed corresponds to a steep incline and high speed corresponds to a flat incline).

   An advantage to viewing human activity in a space–time framework is that it reveals the manner in which a variety of constraints combine to circumscribe the activities in which an individual *can* participate. As originally

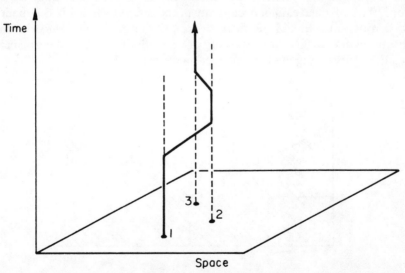

Figure 2–1. Hägerstrand's Space–Time Representation of Human Activity.

conceptualized by Hägerstrand[3] and summarized by Pred,[4] these constraints include:

1. *Capability constraints* that circumscribe behavior by demanding large blocks of time for physiological necessities (sleeping, eating, and personal care) and by limiting the distances an individual can travel within a particular time span in accord with the available transportation system.
2. *Coupling constraints* that pinpoint where, when, and for how long an individual must join other individuals (or objects) in order to participate in production, consumption, social, and other miscellaneous activities.
3. *Authority constraints* that determine who does and does not have access to specific domains at specific times to do specific things as a result of general rules, laws, economic barriers, and power relationships.

These three general categories of constraints result from the fundamental facts that individuals are indivisible (that is, no person can be at two or more places simultaneously); movement is always time consuming; every activity has a duration; every situation is inevitably rooted in past situations; and space has a limited packing capacity.[5]

To exemplify how these constraints work together to delineate behavioral spaces, consider an individual's situation when he is constrained to be located at some point r_1 until time t_1 and has transportation available which allows travel in all directions at a maximum velocity v. Under these conditions, the individual cannot occupy any of the points included in the shaded portion of space-time depicted in figure 2–2 (space is represented in one dimension in this figure for simplicity of exposition). He cannot participate in any activity taking place in this portion of space-time.

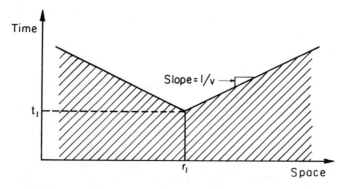

Figure 2–2. Space–Time Diagram for Individual Confronted with an Origin Coupling Constraint.

Without any further constraints, the individual would have available an unlimited set of trajectories through the unshaded portion of space-time in figure 2-2. However, the case of not having to arrive at some predetermined location at some predetermined time is extremely rare. Thus the individual's behavioral space is delineated further by the existence of a destination coupling constraint. This is depicted in figure 2-3, where the individual is constrained to arrive at some point r_2 by time t_2 (for example, r_2 could be the individual's work location and t_2 his work starting time). The origin coupling constraint (r_1, t_1), the destination coupling constraint (r_2, t_2), and the maximum speed v together define what Hägerstrand refers to as a space-time "prism." Points inside the prism can be occupied by the individual. Thus the prism defines all possible paths or trajectories in space-time which are available to the individual between the times t_1 and t_2. Furthermore, as described in figure 2-4, the prism defines the locations an individual can reach, the maximum amounts of time that he can spend at these locations, the distance to each location from r_1 and from r_2, and the travel time from r_1 to each location and from each location to r_2.

Space-time prisms provide the fundamental building blocks for this study of accessibility. It is important to recognize that the ability to occupy various points in space-time is a necessary but not sufficient condition for being able to participate in activities at these points. This follows because an individual's actual ability to participate in a variety of activities within a space-time prism also depends on the spatial and temporal distributions of activities within this prism, the amounts of time required to participate in different activities, and the authority the individual has to participate in these activities. However, before considering how these latter factors influence accessibility, an understanding is required of how an individual's possible daily paths in space-time are delineated.

Within Hägerstrand's framework, the possible daily paths in space-time available to an individual are circumscribed by a set of space-time

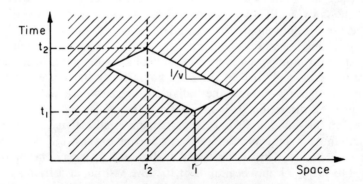

Figure 2-3. Space-Time Diagram for Individual Confronted with Origin and Destination Coupling Constraints.

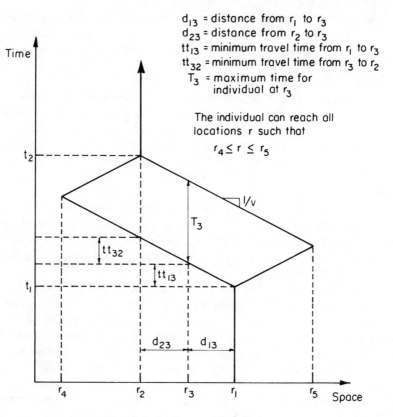

Figure 2-4. Space-Time Prism.

prisms linked together by a set of coupling constraints. Consider, for example, the simplistic case of a sample individual constrained to be at home each day from 10 P.M. until 6 A.M. (This constraint could result from the individual's own physiological needs or the needs of other members of his household.) If this individual is not confronted with additional coupling constraints and has transportation available that allows travel at a maximum speed v, he is capable of selecting paths in space-time between 6 A.M. and 10 P.M. that are bounded by the space-time prism depicted in figure 2-5. How the individual behaves each day within this prism is at his discretion. It is important to recognize, however, that any decision on the individual's part to participate in an activity at some location and time for some duration renders a portion of the original space-time prism inaccessible. This is illustrated in figure 2-6, where the individual decided to spend 3 hours beginning at 10 A.M. visiting at a friend's home. The opportunity cost of participating in this activity is represented by the shaded portion of the prism.

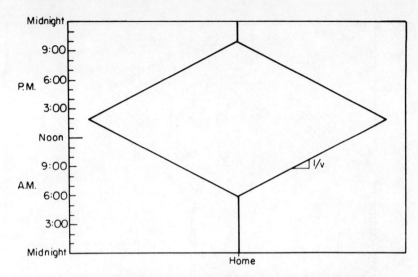

Figure 2-5. Space-Time Prism of an Individual Constrained to Be at Home from 10 P.M. to 6 A.M.

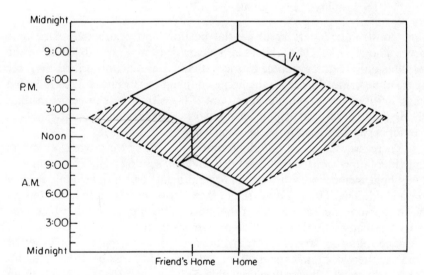

Figure 2-6. Opportunity Costs in Space-Time When an Individual Decides to Participate in an Activity.

Now consider the case of a sample individual confronted with additional coupling constraints. Assume, for example, that the individual is employed at a location 20 miles away from 8 A.M. until 12 noon and from 1 P.M. until 5 P.M. As shown in figure 2-7, the imposition of this space-

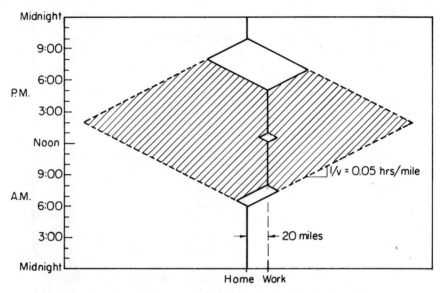

Figure 2-7. Example of the Daily Space-Time Prisms Available to an
Employed Individual.

time constraint renders a substantial portion of the original space-time
prism inaccessible. (The individual's velocity is v = 20 mi/h.) Here the
possible daily paths available to the individual are circumscribed by three
space-time prisms linked by the home coupling constraint and the morning
and afternoon work coupling constraints. It is within these three prisms that
the individual can participate in nonwork activities and activities which
cannot be performed at home between 6 A.M. and 10 P.M.

There are numerous coupling constraints other than work which an
individual may confront. Examples include school, delivering another
household member to and from an appointment, or being at home to care
for a child. The coupling constraints faced by a specific individual depend
on the personal characteristics of the individual (that is, whether he or she
works, attends school, has children, and his or her sex, age, and so on).
These coupling constraints fix individuals at points in space for periods of
time and therefore render portions of space-time inaccessible to the individual. Furthermore, the resulting possible paths in space-time available to an
individual can be represented by sets of space-time prisms linked by coupling constraints.

This study is concerned with how a variety of transportation, temporal,
and spatial strategies impact individuals' accessibilities by affecting the
paths in space-time *available* to them. The following chapter provides
examples of these strategies and a discussion of their accessibility implications in the context of Hägerstrand's paradigm.

3 The Space–Time Implications of Transportation, Temporal, and Spatial Strategies

As illustrated in the previous chapter, Hägerstrand's space–time representation of human activity diagrammatically reveals the spatial and temporal characteristics of behavioral constraints. This chapter uses Hägerstrand's representation to examine the spatial and temporal implications of a variety of strategies affecting these behavioral constraints. These strategies affect either (1) the coupling constraints an individual confronts, or (2) the transportation available to an individual (either the transportation network or the speed that the network can be traversed). Examples of strategies generating these two types of impacts and discussions of their accessibility implications follow.

Strategies Affecting Coupling Constraints

Coupling constraints fix individuals at points in space for periods of time. Any strategy that either (1) provides an individual with discretion over the exact time period they must occupy a particular point in space, (2) changes the amount of time a point must be occupied, (3) changes the point in space that the individual must occupy for a period of time, or (4) eliminates a coupling constraint altogether will change the coupling constraints an individual confronts. Table 3-1 provides examples of each of these types of strategies. A discussion of these examples follows.

Flexible working hours, typically referred to as *flextime*, is an example of the first type of strategy. To illustrate the impact of flextime on an individual's space–time autonomy, recall the simplistic case depicted in figure 2-7. There an individual is free to depart from home each morning at 6 A.M. and can sustain a maximum speed of $v = 20$ mi/h. This individual must begin work at 8 A.M. at a location 20 miles from home. He has an hour off for lunch (from 12 noon to 1 P.M.) and must remain at work until 5 P.M. The individual must return home by 10 P.M.

Now suppose this individual's employer instituted a flextime program. Under this program, all employees are still required to work 8 hours a day. However, rather than having to be at work from 8 A.M. to 12 noon and from 1 P.M. to 5 P.M., the employer now requires them to be at work only from 9 A.M. to 12 noon and 1 P.M. to 4 P.M. This allows the individual to

Table 3-1
Examples of Strategies Affecting Coupling Constraints

Impact of Strategy	Example
Provides discretion over period of time a point must be occupied.	Flextime, extending hours for post offices and banks, night education programs.
Changes the amount of time a point must be occupied.	Shortened work day, fast-food restaurants, microwave oven.
Changes point in space an individual must occupy for a period of time.	Zoning, public facility location decisions, housing policies.
Eliminates a coupling constraint.	Providing day care centers, school bus service, videotape recorders, timers on ovens.

begin work as early as 7 A.M. or as late as 9 A.M. and, depending on what time he begins, finish work as early as 4 P.M. or as late as 6 P.M. The portion of space-time which the individual has discretion over each day when flextime is available is depicted in figure 3-1. The space-time prisms available prior to flextime are superimposed on this figure. The shaded portion of space-time represents the increase in space-time autonomy that the individual gains from flextime.

Figure 3-1 can be misleading without a clear understanding of the opportunity costs associated with the individual's decision when to work. Each day the individual has the option to select paths in space-time that are circumscribed by the larger prisms depicted in figure 3-1. However, by exercising his option to start work later than 8 A.M. or finish work earlier than 5 P.M., he reduces the size of his space-time prism after work or before work, respectively. The two extreme options available to the individual are depicted in figures 3-2 and 3-3. The space-time prisms available to the individual prior to flextime are superimposed on these two figures.

Observe that by starting work at 7 A.M. rather than 8 A.M., the individual incurs an opportunity cost represented by the cross-hatched portion of space-time in figure 3-2. However, this opportunity cost is traded off against an increase in space-time autonomy represented by the dotted portion of space-time in the same figure. If the individual started work at 9 A.M. instead of 8 A.M., the cross-hatched portion of space-time in figure 3-3 would represent the opportunity cost and the dotted portion of space-time would represent the increase in space-time autonomy.

Figures 3-2 and 3-3 illustrate how flextime allows individuals to piece together larger blocks of time to participate in activities at different locations either before or after work. Furthermore, they illustrate how flextime provides individuals with the opportunity to spend time at more locations and to occupy locations at times that were not possible prior to flextime. Such changes could, for example, make it possible for the individual to visit

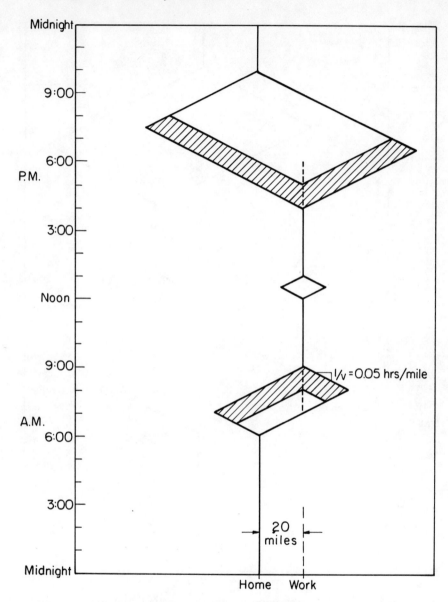

Figure 3–1. Daily Space–Time Autonomy of an Individual with Flextime.

a dentist or doctor without missing work or have enough daylight to play golf either before or after work. A general discussion of the importance of the number and sizes of the blocks of time available to individuals is provided by Hummon.[1]

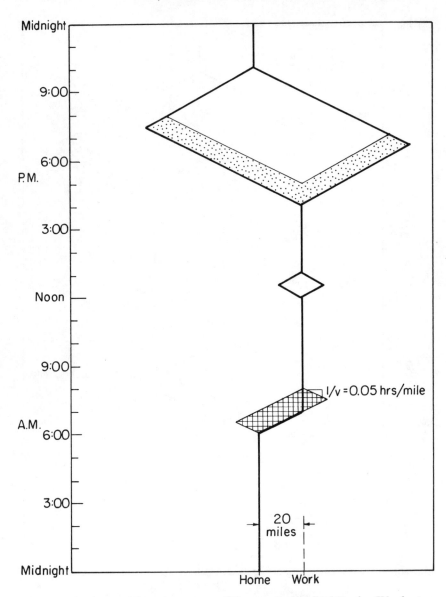

Figure 3-2. Space-Time Autonomy When an Individual Begins Work at
7 A.M.

Examples of other strategies that provide an individual with discretion
over the exact time period he or she must occupy a particular location
include extending the service hours of banks or post offices, keeping stores
open longer, and offering night education. All these strategies affect the

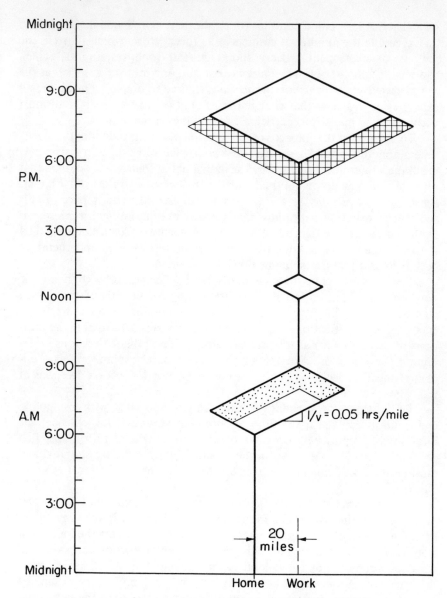

Figure 3-3. Space–Time Autonomy When an Individual Begins Work at
          9 A.M.

temporal distribution of activities and therefore provide an individual with
more discretion over when a desired or necessary activity can be performed.

The second way coupling constraints can be modified is by changing the
amount of time an individual must occupy a point in order to participate in

an activity. A new union contract which shortens an individual's work day; an increase in the number of cashiers at a grocery store, which shortens the amount of time spent grocery shopping; fast-food restaurants, which shorten the amount of time required to eat out; and innovations such as the microwave oven, which shorten the time required to prepare a meal, are all examples of strategies that change the amount of time an individual must occupy a point in order to participate in activities at that point.

To exemplify the impacts of these changes on an individual's space-time autonomy, consider the case of a shortened work day. In particular, recall the situation confronted by the individual in figure 2-1. Assume that because of a new union contract, this individual now works only 7 hours, finishing the work day at 4 P.M. instead of 5 P.M. The impact of this shortened work day on the individual's space-time autonomy is represented by the shaded area in figure 3-4. With a shortened work day, the individual is free to spend larger amounts of time at more locations and therefore occupy locations at times that he previously could not.

The third way coupling constraints can be changed is by changing the points in space that an individual must occupy for periods of time. Such changes could result from land-use strategies (zoning or other strategies encouraging densification or sprawl); public decisions determining the locations of facilities such as schools and post offices; private decisions determining the locations of employment centers or shopping centers; residential-location decisions of households; or the work-location decisions of individuals.

To illustrate how a change in the location associated with a coupling constraint affects the space-time autonomy of an individual, consider the locations of employment opportunities for an individual with a specified residential location. Recall again the case in figure 2-7. There an individual must be at work 20 miles away from 8 A.M. to 12 noon and from 1 P.M. to 5 P.M.

Now suppose that a comparable employment opportunity is made available to the individual at a location only 5 miles away in the same direction. Figure 3-5 depicts the changes in space-time autonomy the individual would experience by taking the closer job. The dotted portion of space-time encompasses those points available to the individual at the closer job location which are not available at the original job location. The cross-hatched portion of space-time encompasses those points available to the individual when he works at the original job location which are not available when he works at the closer job location. It is interesting to note that the dotted portion of space-time includes the opportunities for the individual to spend an additional 45 minutes at home each morning and evening as well as a half hour at home during his lunch break.

The final way to change the coupling constraints individuals confront is to eliminate one or more coupling constraints altogether. Coupling constraints can be eliminated through

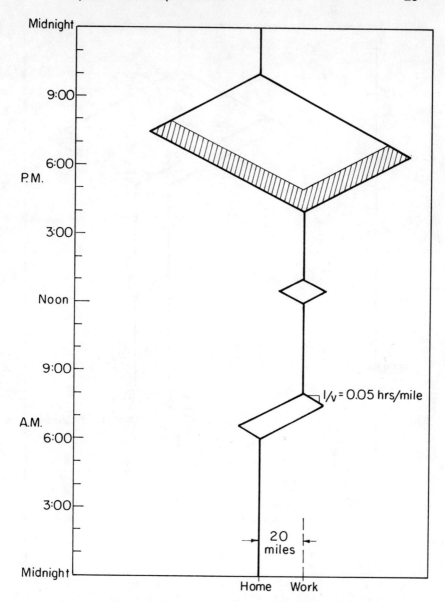

Figure 3–4. Impact of Shortened Work Day on an Individual's Daily
Space–Time Autonomy.

1. Provision of day care centers in order to free parents from being at
   home to care for children.
2. Provision of school bus service in order to free parents from trans-
   porting their children to and from school.

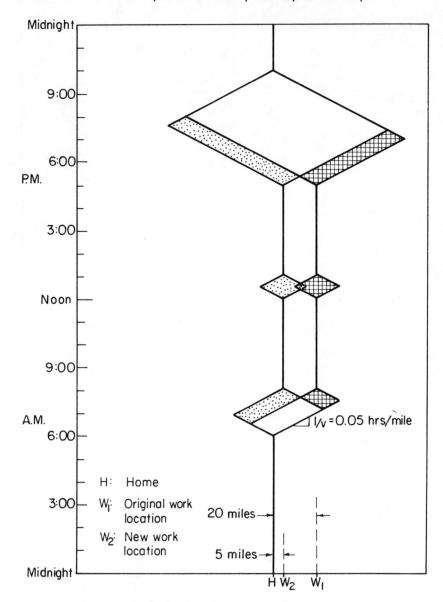

Figure 3–5. Impact of a Closer Work Location on an Individual's Daily
Space–Time Autonomy.

3. Innovations such as video tape recorders which allow television pro-
grams to be recorded for viewing at a later time.
4. Timers on ovens which allow a meal to begin cooking without someone
being present at home to turn on the oven.

To exemplify the impact of eliminating a coupling constraint on an individual's space-time autonomy, consider a parent who is free to leave home at 8 A.M., must pick up his child at school 2 miles from home at 2 P.M., and must return home by 4 P.M. to prepare dinner. He has transportation available which allows travel at a maximum speed $v = 20$ mi/h. The space-time autonomy of this parent is depicted in figure 3-6.

Now if the school system provided school bus service to transport the child from school to home, the parent would no longer have to pick up the child. The parent's space-time autonomy would be expanded as depicted in figure 3-7. The original space-time autonomy of the parent is superimposed on figure 3-7. The shaded portion of space-time in this figure represents the increased space-time autonomy of the parent.

Strategies Affecting Transportation

The transportation available to individuals in part determines the geometries of their space-time prisms. Underlying the space-time prisms discussed so far is the supposition that an individual is capable of traveling at a constant maximum speed in all directions and at all times. Clearly, this is a very idealized view of an individual's ability to overcome space. In reality,

1. The paths in geographical space that an individual can traverse are typically constrained to a network that does not allow equal speed of travel in all directions.
2. The maximum speed at which an individual can traverse a network varies with the time of day and the individual's location on the network (because congestion and mode availability may vary with the time of day and because the capacities of links and speed limits on links may vary over a network).
3. Certain modes are tied to routes and/or schedules and therefore impose additional coupling constraints on individuals who rely on them.

It is unrealistic (and unnecessary) to attempt to accurately depict all the realities of transportation in a space-time framework. However, these realities can be idealistically depicted in a space-time framework to reflect the essence of how they shape behavioral spaces and, therefore, how different transportation strategies influence the space-time autonomies of individuals.

From the standpoint of an individual, transportation strategies can be viewed as either influencing (1) the speeds at which modes can operate, (2) the extent and geometry of the networks over which modes operate, (3) the routing and scheduling of modes, or (4) the availability of modes (for example, whether an individual has an automobile available). This study

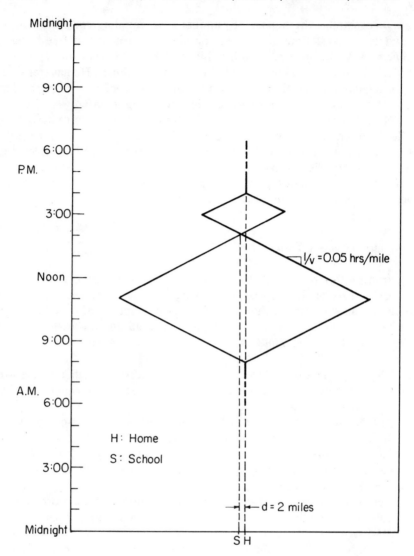

Figure 3-6. Daily Space-Time Autonomy of Parent Constrained to Pick
        Pick Up Child at School.

concentrates on the accessibility impacts of the first two types of strategies.
Consequently, modes are assumed to always be available to individuals
independent of their location and the time of day. An examination of how
accessibility varies with the routing and scheduling of modes and the availability of modes is relegated to future research.

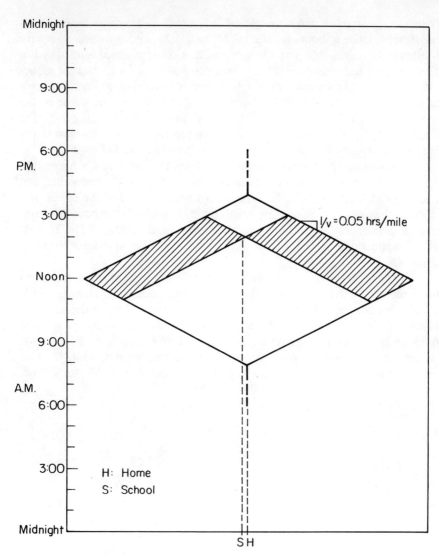

Figure 3–7. Impact of Eliminating a Coupling Constraint on an Individual's Space–Time Autonomy.

Speed limit restrictions, increases in capacity to reduce congestion, exclusive lanes for high-occupancy vehicles, and ramp metering are all examples of strategies which influence the maximum speeds individuals can expect to sustain using different modes. To exemplify the nature of the impacts such strategies have on the space–time autonomies of individuals, return to the simple situation depicted in figure 2–5. There an individual is constrained to be at home from 10 P.M. to 6 A.M. and is assumed to have transportation available that allows travel at a constant maximum speed in all directions and at all times. Now consider the case of a 25 percent reduction in an individual's maximum speed (such a reduction could be necessitated by an energy crisis). This reduction in speed changes the shape of the space–time prism available to the individual, as depicted in figure 3–8. The shaded portion of space–time in this figure represents the reduction in the individual's space–time autonomy resulting from the speed change.

Observe that the farther a location is from the individual's home, the greater is the reduction in the maximum amount of time the individual can spend at this location. It is also important to recognize that the effect of a velocity change on a space–time prism depends on both the coupling constraints corresponding to the prism and the original velocity.[2] The accessibility implications of changes in velocity are explored in greater detail in chapter 5.

The assumption that an individual's maximum speed is constant at all times can be relaxed to highlight the accessibility impacts of strategies aimed at reducing congestion. Consider an individual who is free to depart from home each morning at 6 A.M., must arrive at work 20 miles away by 8 A.M., must remain at work until 5 P.M., and must return home by 10 P.M. Assume that this individual can travel at a maximum speed of 30 mi/h at all times except from 7:30 A.M. to 9 A.M. and from 4:30 P.M. to 6 P.M.

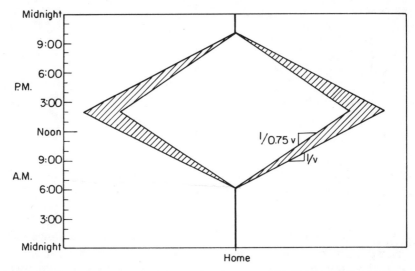

Figure 3–8. Effect of a Velocity Reduction on an Individual's Space–Time Autonomy.

During these two periods, congestion exists which reduces the individual's maximum speed to 20 mi/h. While instantaneous congestion is unrealistic, it is assumed here for purposes of illustration.

This individual's space–time autonomy is depicted in figure 3–9. Observe that the different velocities are reflected by different slopes of the

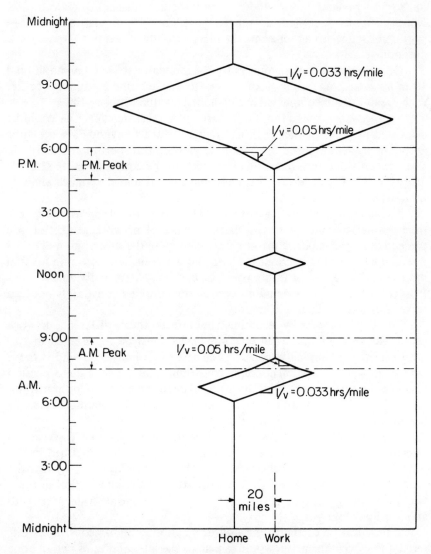

Figure 3–9. Effect of Congestion on an Individual's Space–Time Autonomy.

trajectories bounding the individual's space–time prisms. Also note that the individual has the option of avoiding congestion by arriving at work early and leaving work late.

Now consider the impact of a strategy that seeks to expand capacity to the point where congestion is eliminated. Such a strategy would allow the individual to travel at 30 mi/h at all times. Figure 3–10 depicts the individual's space–time autonomy under these new conditions. The previous case, where congestion existed, is superimposed on this figure. The shaded portion of space–time represents the increase in the individual's space–time autonomy.

Observe that the opportunities for the individual to spend an additional 10 minutes at home each morning and to arrive home 20 minutes earlier each evening are encompassed in the shaded portion of space–time.

Figure 3–10 suggests that the benefits of increasing capacities could be evaluated in terms of the resulting changes in the individual's space–time autonomies. As discussed in chapter 1, viewing transportation benefits in this way provides an interesting alternative to the conventional method of assessing benefits in terms of travel-time savings and the values analysts impute from these savings.

To illustrate how physical networks affect behavioral spaces, the space–time prisms associated with two extreme types of network geometries are presented. In particular, a prism corresponding to the case of an individual who can travel in all directions is compared with one in which an individual must travel on a fine–grid network. In both cases, the individual is confronted with the same origin and destination coupling constraints and can travel at the same maximum speed.

To diagrammatically examine the effects these different network geometries have on space–time prisms, space must be represented in two dimensions. For simplicity, consider the case of an individual who is faced with origin and destination coupling constraints that have the same location (as in figure 2–5). In particular, let (x, y, t_1) be the origin coupling constraint and (x, y, t_2) be the destination coupling constraint. Furthermore, let v be the maximum speed the individual can travel in both cases.

The resulting space–time prism when the individual can travel in all directions is depicted in figure 3–11. This prism is a volume defined by the intersection of two identical cones, one with its apex at (x, y, t_1) and the other with its apex at (x, y, t_2). The projection of the intersection of these two cones onto geographical space forms a circle having an origin at $(x, y, 0)$ and a radius of $(t_2 - t_1/2)v$.

If the location of the origin and destination coupling constraints differed, the space–time prism would appear as the intersection of two oblique

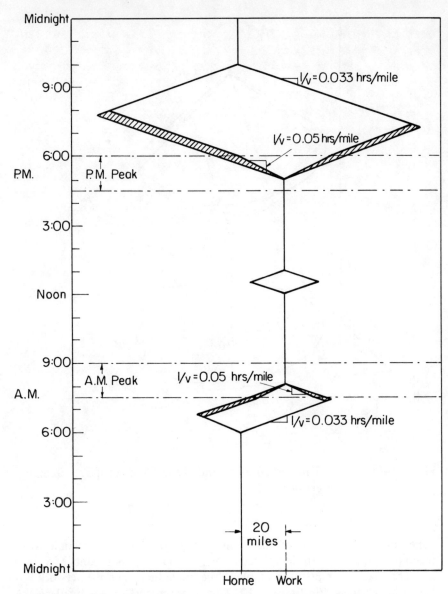

Figure 3–10. Impact of Eliminating Peak–Period Congestion on an Individual's Space–Time Autonomy.

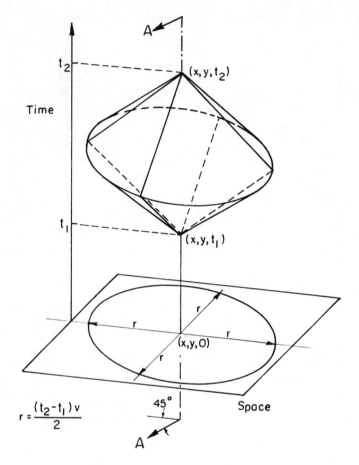

Figure 3-11. Space–Time Prism for an Individual Capable of Traveling in
All Directions.

cones, and the projection of this prism onto geographical space would form
an ellipse with foci at the locations of the two coupling constraints.[3]

The space–time prism available to the individual when the network is a
fine grid is depicted in figure 3-12. This prism is a volume defined by the
intersection of two identical pyramids with apexes at (x, y, t_1) and (x, y, t_2).
The projection of the intersection of these pyramids onto geographical
space forms a square. The diagonal of this square has length $(t_2 - t_1)v$.

Figures 3-13 and 3-14 depict the nature of the differences in the space–
time prisms corresponding to the two extreme network geometries.[4] Figure

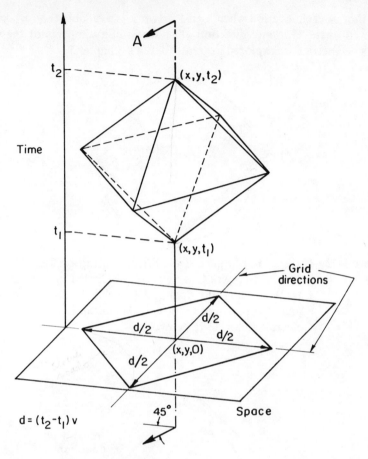

Figure 3–12. Space–Time Prism for an Individual Constrained to Traveling on an Fine–Grid Network.

3–13 compares the projection of each prism onto geographical space. It is obvious that fewer locations can be reached when the individual is constrained to a grid than when he is allowed to travel in all directions. Figure 3–14 represents the intersection of each space–time prism with a plane that is parallel to the time axis and intersects space at a 45° angle to the directions of the paths of the fine–grid network. This plane is represented by the section *A–A* in both figure 3–11 and figure 3–12. As expected, it takes longer for the individual to reach locations when traveling on a grid than when traveling directly to each point. Therefore, the individual can spend less time at each location when a grid network is available than when he is allowed to travel in any direction. The accessibility impacts of these network geometries are explored in greater detail in chapter 5.

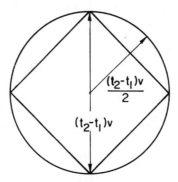

Figure 3–13. Projections of Space–Time Prisms Corresponding to Different Network Geometries. The Circle Corresponds to the Case Where an Individual Can Travel in All Directions. The Square Corresponds to the Case Where an Individual Is Constrained to a Grid Network.

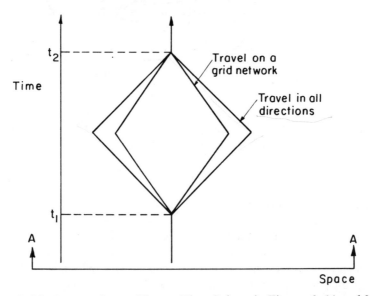

Figure 3–14. Intersections of Space–Time Prisms in Figures 3–11 and 3–12 with a Plane Parallell to the Time Axis and Intersecting Space at a 45° Angle to the Directions of the Paths of the Grid Network.

4 Benefits of Space–Time Autonomy

The preceding discussion illustrates how a variety of strategies affect the space–time autonomies of individuals. To compare the effects of these different strategies, the benefits that individuals derive from changes in their space–time autonomies must be assessed. To accomplish this end, a variety of *accessibility-benefit measures* are proposed based on different *idealized assumptions* regarding how individuals *might value* their space–time autonomies. This approach allows different strategies to be assessed and compared from different perspectives on individual's valuations.

Underlying the accessibility–benefit measures proposed here is the supposition that, all other things being equal, the larger the space–time prisms of individuals, the better off they are. This is consistent with the argument (outlined in chapter 1) that accessibility is valued highly by individuals and that public policy should be providing individuals with a greater opportunity to realize their desires and should be distributing these opportunities more equitably. However, equating greater benefits with larger space–time prisms and therefore more accessibility to individuals must be qualified in three ways.[1]

First, the concept of accessibility benefit, as conceived here, pertains to individuals and not to society as a whole. While an individual may benefit from having greater accessibility, it is not clear whether society as a whole benefits. This follows because the effects on other individuals of increasing one individual's accessibility are not clearly defined. Therefore, an increase in an individual's accessibility may not be beneficial to society in a Pareto sense.

Second, it is possible that an increase in the accessibilities of individuals at one point in time may, in the long run, result in a net reduction in their accessibilities. For example, the automobile is widely recognized as an accessibility–enhancing technology. However, accompanying the growth of automobile systems in developed countries are changes in the spatial distribution of activities. It is not clear whether the automobile functioning in spatial environments that evolved with the automobile system, provides more accessibility to individuals than, for example, public transportation would provide in spatial environments conducive to public transportation systems.

Finally, arguing that enlarging the space–time prisms of individuals is beneficial does not consider "option" values[2] of land and other resources.

Specifically, enhancing one's access to limited resources today may reduce the opportunity of future generations to use these resources. This confronts the logic of continually striving to enhance the capabilities of individuals to recognize their desires. It does not, however, diminish the importance of equitably distributing existing capabilities and the need for accessibility-benefit measures to assess these distributions.

In light of these important caveats, two general approaches to measuring accessibility benefits are now developed. Both approaches define a set of opportunities delineated by a space–time prism available to an individual, the value to this individual of each opportunity within this set, and the overall value the individual derives from the entire set.

The basic difference between the two approaches lies in the definition of an opportunity underlying each. The first approach defines an *opportunity* in terms of the attributes of a location, the distance an individual must travel to reach this location, and the amount of time the individual can spend at this location. The second approach defines an *opportunity* in terms of a route (that is, a path through geographical space defined in terms of a sequence of locations), the length of this route, the attributes of each location accessed by this route, and the total amount of time an individual has available to spend at these locations. The remainder of this chapter develops the two general approaches to measuring accessibility-benefits considered here.

Location–Opportunity Approach

The first general type of accessibility-benefit measure is similar in form to measures of *spatial opportunity,* generically referred to as *spatial–accessibility measures.*[3] An implicit assumption underlying conventional spatial-accessibility measures is that individuals value being able to reach a location independent of the precise times or amount of time they can occupy this location. By assuming that individuals value a spatial opportunity relative to the amount of time they *can* spend pursuing this opportunity, the measures proposed here begin to capture the temporal dependence of accessibility. These proposed measures are simple examples of a more general class of measures which assume that individuals value being able to occupy locations relative to the activities available at these locations *during the precise times they can occupy them.*

A general framework for this first type of accessibility-benefit measure is now developed in the context of space-time prisms. Recall that these prisms circumscribe the points in space-time that an individual *can* occupy and still satisfy the coupling constraints he confronts. Any space-time prism can be described in terms of these points. Specifically, consider an individual who is free to leave location i at time t_i and must arrive at location j by time t_j .

Let v = the maximum speed the individual can travel (assumed constant for all locations and times)

d_{ik} = the shortest distance from origin i to some location k

d_{jk} = the shortest distance from destination j to location k

d_k = $d_{ik} + d_{jk}$ (the shortest distance from i to j through k)

a_k = a finite nonnegative real number representing a vector of attributes characterizing location k (for example, levels of activity or facility capacities)

Since geographical space is being considered here in two dimensions, the distances just defined all depend on the network the individual is constrained to travel on.

The space–time prism corresponding to these conditions, denoted here as P, is defined as the set of all points (k, t) in space–time such that

$$t \geq t_i + \frac{d_{ik}}{v} \tag{4.1}$$

and

$$t \leq t_j - \frac{d_{jk}}{v} \tag{4.2}$$

Observe that the surface of P is defined by the points (k, t) wherein either the equality holds in equation 4.1 and the inequality holds in equation 4.2 or the equality holds in equation 4.2 and the inequality holds in equation 4.1. Furthermore, observe that the geographical region encompassing all the locations that the individual can reach and still satisfy the coupling constraints he confronts is defined by the locations k such that

$$d_k \leq (t_j - t_i)v \tag{4.3}$$

Note that the righthand side of equation 4.3 is simply the total distance the individual can travel in the time available between the coupling constraints he confronts.

Denote the geographical region defined by equation 4.3 as R. The boundary of R is defined by locations k where the equality in equation 4.3 holds. These are also the locations where the equalities in both equations 4.1 *and* 4.2 hold.

Finally, observe that the period of time the individual can occupy location k is defined by the times t such that

$$t_i + \frac{d_{ik}}{v} \leq t \leq t_j - \frac{d_{jk}}{v} \qquad (4.4)$$

Define the duration of this period as T_k, where

$$T_k = (t_j - t_i) - \frac{d_k}{v} \qquad (4.5)$$

Each location $k \in R$ can now be characterized by three finite nonnegative numbers: d_k, a_k, and T_k. An ordered triad of these three numbers, denoted (d, a, T), is called a *location opportunity*. This is analogous to the terminology developed by Smith,[4] who has related spatial–interaction models to spatial–choice theory.

Denote the set of all such location opportunities defined by the space–time prism P as

$$C_P = \{(d_k, a_k, T_k) \mid k \in R\} \qquad (4.6)$$

An accessibility-benefit measure relative to P (abbreviated BM_P) is defined in terms of C_P. Specifically, this measure is a function that attributes to any set C_P a finite and nonnegative real number $f(C_P)$. A variety of measures are possible, each corresponding to assumptions regarding the value an individual derives from each opportunity and the subsequent values he derives from a set of opportunities.

Accessibility-benefit measures are defined here in a manner analogous to the way Weibull[5] defines an attraction–accessibility measure (abbreviated AM). The primary difference is that Weibull defines an opportunity in terms of the attraction of a location a and the distance d to this location, while the definition of an opportunity here also includes the amount of time T an individual can spend at this location.

Having defined an opportunity in this way, Weibull proceeds to specify a set of axioms which express basic properties of an AM. He then presents a set of lemmas and a theorem which lead to a general mathematical form for an AM. This mathematical form consists of a function z which attributes a value to each opportunity (d, a) (denoted as a standard–distance substitution formula by Weibull) and a binary operation (for example addition and maximization) which specifies the manner in which the values of the opportunities are combined to determine the overall value attached to the set of opportunities (denoted as a composition rule by Weibull).

Here the location attributes a and the duration T of an opportunity together determine the *attraction* of an opportunity. Specifically, let

$$\sigma = w(a, T) \qquad\qquad (4.7)$$

represent this attraction,

where $w:R_+^2 \to R_+$

> w is continuous
> w is increasing in a and T
> $w(0, T) = 0$
> $w(a, 0) = 0$

Defining an attraction measure in this manner allows an opportunity (d, a, T) to be represented in terms of only two nonnegative finite numbers (d, σ). This is analogous to Weibull's conceptualization of an opportunity. The critical difference is that Weibull defines the attraction of an opportunity solely in terms of the attributes of the location of an opportunity, while σ also depends on the amount of time an individual can spend at this location.

With the preceding distinction in mind, the general form of f defining a BM can be derived in the same manner that Weibull derives the general form of f for an AM. The differences in these general forms is manifested in Weibull's standard–distance substitution function z. For an AM, z is defined as a function of d and a only. For a BM, z is defined as a function of d, a, and T.

The specific axioms, lemmas, and theorems underlying the general mathematical form developed here closely parallel those underlying Weibull's general form. Therefore, only the essential characteristics of the present general form are stated. These characteristics are included in two categories: (1) those related to the value an individual may derive from a single–location opportunity, denoted by $z(d, a, T)$, and (2) those related to the manner in which these discrete opportunity values are combined to determine the overall value an individual may derive from a set of opportunities. Characteristics of $z(d, a, T)$ include the following:

1. For fixed a and T, $z(d, a, T)$ does not increase with increasing d.
2. For fixed d and T, $z(d, a, T)$ does not decrease with increasing a.
3. For fixed d and a, $z(d, a, T)$ does not decrease with increasing T.
4. $\lim_{d \to \infty} z(d, a, T) = 0$
5. $z(d, a, 0) = 0$.
6. $z(d, 0, T) = 0$.
7. $z(d, a, T)$ is independent of the presence of other opportunities

Characteristics of the manner in which the discrete values associated with members of a set of opportunities are combined to determine a benefit measure are encompassed in the following equation:

$$f[C_P] = G[(d_1, a_1, T_1) \oplus \cdots \oplus z(d_n, a_n, T_n)] \qquad (4.8)$$

Here, G is a continuous and increasing function satisfying $G(0) = 0$, $\oplus$ is a binary operation, and n is the number of opportunities in C_P.

An example of a benefit measure satisfying the characteristics just listed is

$$f[(d_k, a_k, T_k)_{k \in R}] = \sum_{k \in R} q(d_k) a_k u(T_k) \qquad (4.9)$$

where q is a nonincreasing function that is unity for $d_k = 0$, and u is a nondecreasing function that is zero for $T_k = 0$. In this example

$$z(d_k, a_k, T_k) = q(d_k) a_k u(T_k) \qquad (4.10)$$

the binary operation $\oplus$ is arithmetic addition, and G is such that $G(x) = x$. Another example is

$$f[(d_k, a_k, T_k)_{k \in R}] = \max [q(d_k) a_k u(T_k)]_{k \in R} \qquad (4.11)$$

In this case, z and G are specified as in the previous example, and the binary operation $\oplus$ is the max operation. This measure assumes that the benefit an individual derives from a set of opportunities is equivalent to the benefit he derives from the opportunity in the set which has the greatest value.

Route–Opportunity Approach

The second general type of accessibility–benefit measure considered is based on opportunities defined in terms of routes. A *route* is a path through geographical space. Defining opportunities in terms of routes is more realistic in a behavioral sense than defining opportunities in terms of locations. However, it is conceptually and analytically more complex.

Like the location–opportunity approach, the route–opportunity approach develops accessibility–benefit measures in the context of a space-time prism. Again, consider an individual who is free to leave location i at time t_i and must arrive at location j at time t_j.

Let v = the maximum speed the individual can travel (assumed constant for all locations and times)

a_k = a finite nonnegative real number representing a vector of attributes characterizing location k (for example, levels of activity or facility capacities)

R = the geographical region defined by the space-time prism available to the individual (as defined in equation 4.3)

When locations are viewed discretely, a route can be described in terms of the set of locations accessed by the route and the order in which these locations are accessed. Since there is a finite number of locations within R, there is a finite number of routes within R that originate at location i and terminate at location j. This number of routes depends on the network connecting locations within R.

Because a route is characterized in part by the order in which it accesses locations, a given subset of locations in R can correspond to more than one route. However, since temporal distributions of activities are not considered in this study, the order in which a route accesses locations is not important here. As such, a route can be uniquely characterized in terms of the set of locations it accesses and the *minimum* distance from origin i to destination j through each location in this set.

Let L = set of locations $k \in R$ accessed by a specific route

x_L = the minimum distance from origin i to destination j through each location $k \in L$.

The amount of time it would take the individual to travel route L is x_L/v. Because of the space-time constraints confronted by the individual, he can consider only the subset of routes L defined by R wherein

$$x_L/v < t_j - t_i \qquad (4.12)$$

If the individual traveled route L, he would be able to spend an amount of time

$$\bar{s}_L = t_j - t_i - x_L/v \qquad (4.13)$$

stopped at the locations $k \in L$. Each possible allocation of the amount of time $\bar{s}_L$ to these locations uniquely defines a trajectory. Because time is a continuous variable, there are an infinite number of possible time allocations and therefore trajectories corresponding to each route L. As such, attempting to define a finite set of opportunities in terms of trajectories is conceptually impossible. (Chapter 5 addresses the question of individuals allocating time to locations in greater depth.)

Opportunities can, however, be defined in terms of routes. Specifically, for each route L within R that the individual can traverse (that is, each L

such that the inequality in equation 4.12 holds), the individual has the opportunity of allocating the amount of time $\bar{s}_L$ over the set of locations $k \in L$. Each location in this set is characterized by a vector of attributes.

Let $\bar{a}$ = a finite nonnegative number representing an aggregation of the vectors of the attributes corresponding to each location $k \in L$.

Each route L that the individual can traverse can now be characterized by three finite nonnegative numbers: x_L, $\bar{a}_L$, $\bar{s}_L$. An ordered triad of these numbers, denoted $(x, \bar{a}, \bar{s})$, is called a *route opportunity*. Notice that a route opportunity is analogous to a location opportunity in which all activities along a route are located at a single location a distance x away. This analogy highlights an important issue concerning the practical definition of the numbers of a_k and $\bar{a}_L$. Consider, for example, the activity "shopping for food." A location k could be defined to be the location of a grocery store, and the number a_k could represent the attributes of this store. However, location k could be defined more precisely as a shelf within the store, and a_k could represent the attributes of the commodities on this shelf. Thus implicit in the definition of a_k is a notion of attribute aggregation. In forming $\bar{a}_L$, an initial set of locations are being aggregated even further. Nevertheless, $\bar{a}_L$ is conceptually the same as a_k.

Denote the set of all route opportunities defined by the space–time prism P as

$$\overline{C}_P = \{(x_L, \bar{a}_L, \bar{s}_L,) \mid x_L/v < t_j - t_i\} \tag{4.14}$$

If the network connecting locations in R allows travel from location i to location j directly through each of these locations without passing through any other location, the set of location opportunities in equation 4.6 is a subset of $\overline{C}_P$. In particular, under this condition the set in equation 4.6 is the set of route opportunities characterized by routes which go directly through a single location where all remaining available time is spent.

An accessibility–benefit measure relative to P can be defined in terms of $\overline{C}_P$. This accessibility–benefit measure is analogous in form to the accessibility–benefit measure defined in terms of location opportunities in equation 4.8. It consists of specifying a function which defines the value an individual may derive from a single route opportunity, denoted by $\bar{z}(x, \bar{a}, \bar{s})$, and a function and operation which determine the manner in which these discrete route–opportunity values are combined to determine the overall value an individual may derive from a set of route opportunities.

The characteristics of $\bar{z}(x, \bar{a}, \bar{s})$ are directly analogous to the seven characteristics of $z(d, a, T)$ listed in the previous section. Similarly, the characteristics of the manner in which the discrete values associated with members of a set of route opportunities are combined to determine a benefit measure are encompassed in an equation directly analogous to equation 4.8. Specifically,

$$f[\overline{C}_P] = H[\overline{z}(x_1, \bar{a}_1 \ \bar{s}_1) \oplus \cdots \oplus \overline{z}(x_m, \bar{a}_m, \bar{s}_m)] \qquad (4.15)$$

where H is a continuous and increasing function satisfying $H(0) = 0$, $\oplus$ is a binary operation, and m is the number of route opportunities in $\overline{C}_P$. Examples of accessibility–benefit measures having the general form of equation 4.15 are measures similar in form to equations 4.9 and 4.11.

Of particular interest here and in chapter 5 are accessibility–benefit measures in which the binary operation in equation 4.15 is the max operation. These measures assume that the value an individual derives from a set of route opportunities is equivalent to the value he derives from the route opportunity with the greatest value in the set. These measures are of particular interest here because they are analogous to the concept in economic consumer theory of an indirect utility function. Economic consumer theory would argue that the route with the greatest value in a set is the route the individual would decide to travel. By equating the value of a set of route opportunities to the value of the route the individual would decide to travel, this theory is inferring value from behavior.

The two proposed approaches to measuring accessibility benefits indicate that these measures depend on the value an individual derives from each opportunity available to him and the manner in which these discrete values are combined to determine the overall value he derives from a set of opportunities. As such, accessibility–benefit measures are subjective; that is, they are based on assumptions regarding the valuations of individuals. This points to the necessity of evaluating different accessibility–enhancing strategies using a variety of measures based on different perspectives regarding the valuations of individuals. Such evaluations are provided in the following chapter.

5

Analytical Comparisons of Different Strategies

Using the two frameworks developed in the previous chapter for measuring the accessibility benefits individuals may derive from changes in their space-time autonomy, the effects of strategies initiating such changes can be evaluated and compared. This is accomplished in the context of a number of simple cases which develop and analyze a variety of accessibility-benefit measures based on different perspectives, on individuals' valuations, and on a wide range of idealized conditions (such as idealized network geometries and activity distributions). Principles result from these simple cases which are applicable when evaluating accessibility-enhancing strategies with respect to complex real-world conditions. These principles lead to general conclusions regarding the relative attractiveness of different strategies.

Specifically, this section compares the effects of strategies that change (1) the velocity an individual can travel, (2) the amount of time between the coupling constraints he confronts, (3) the geometry of the network he is constrained to travel on, and (4) the spatial distribution of activities. These comparisons are made in terms of the effects such strategies have on the space-time autonomy represented by a *single* space-time prism.

Eight cases are analyzed. Case 1 compares strategies that change the velocities individuals can travel, denoted from now on as *velocity strategies,* with strategies that change the amount of time between the coupling constraints individuals confront (that is, their time constraints), denoted from now on as *temporal strategies*. This case highlights the essential difference between the effects these two types of strategies have on the amount of time an individual can spend at different locations. It provides important initial insights regarding the advantage of each type of strategy and sets the stage for the remaining cases.

Cases 2 through 6 evaluate and compare different strategies using benefit measures based on location opportunities and characterized by equation 4.8. Cases 2 and 3 analyze two different network geometries, one allowing travel in all directions and one restricting travel to a fine-grid network. Cases 2, 4, 5, and 6 introduce different specifications of the functions q and u in equation 4.8. The specifications in case 2 implicitly assume that individuals value each differential element of space-time comprising a space-time prism equally. The specifications in case 4 allow the marginal value of the amount of time an individual can spend at the location of a location opportunity to vary. In case 5, the specifications discount the value of a location opportunity with the distance an individual must travel to reach the location of this opportunity. Finally, the specifications in case 6 allow a variety of activity distributions to be considered.

Cases 7 and 8 develop accessibility-benefit measures based on route opportunities and having the general form specified in equation 4.15. Of particular interest in these cases are accessibility-benefit measures specified in a manner analogous to using economic utility theory to develop measures of value. Case 7 considers route opportunities defined over a single geographical path and differing only with respect to the lengths of the routes. In so doing, it focuses on the tradeoffs individuals make when allocating their time between travel (and therefore, accessing locations) and pursuing activities while stopped. Case 8 focuses on decisions of individuals regarding the amounts of time to spend pursuing activities at different locations along a *given* route and the implications of these time-allocation decisions with respect to measuring benefits.

Case 1: Basic Difference between Velocity Strategies and Temporal Strategies

This case examines the sensitivities of the maximum amount of time an individual can spend at different locations to changes in the maximum velocity he can sustain, as well as the amount of time available between the coupling constraints he confronts. Recall the situation developed in the previous section entailing an individual who (1) is free to leave location i at time t_i, (2) must arrive at location j by time t_j, and (3) has a mode available at all times that operates at a constant maximum velocity v. Represent the amount of time available between the coupling constraints this individual confronts as

$$\tau = t_j - t_i \tag{5.1}$$

Assume that v is large enough so that the individual can arrive at j before time t_j, that is,

$$v > d_{ij}/\tau \tag{5.2}$$

The maximum amount of time the individual can spend at location k, T_k, is defined by equation 4.5, which is repeated here for convenience:

$$T_k = \begin{cases} \tau - d_k/v & \text{for all } k \in R \\ 0 & \text{otherwise.} \end{cases} \tag{5.3}$$

The sensitivities of T_k to τ and v are examined in detail. This is done relative to d_k and, therefore, without specifying a transportation network or the distance between i and j.

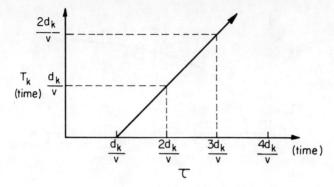

Figure 5-1. T_k versus τ.

It is obvious from equation 5.3 that, (1) if $k \in R$ and τ increases, T_k will increase by an equal amount, and (2) if $k \in R$ and τ decreases, T_k either decreases by an equal amount or decreases to zero. This is depicted in figure 5-1, where $T_k = 0$ for $\tau \leq d_k/v$ and T_k increases linearly for $\tau \geq d_k/v$. Observe that the slope of this linear relationship is 1 for all $\tau \geq d_k/v$, that is,

$$\frac{\partial T_k}{\partial \tau} = 1 \qquad (5.4)$$

Thus, providing $k \in R$, the rate at which the maximum amount of time available at k changes with respect to τ is independent of v, τ, and the precise location of k relative to i and j.

The manner in which T_k varies with v is depicted in figure 5-2, where T_k versus v is plotted. Observe that T_k asymptotically approaches τ as v becomes very large:

$$\lim_{v \to \infty} T_k = \tau \qquad (5.5)$$

Thus no matter how fast the individual can travel, he can never spend more than τ units of time at any location. Furthermore, the rate at which T_k increases with respect to increases in v diminishes as v increases. This is evidenced by examining the manner in which $\partial T_k/\partial v$ varies with v, as shown in figure 5-3. In particular,

$$\frac{\partial T_k}{\partial v} = \frac{d_k}{v^2} \qquad (5.6)$$

and

$$\lim_{v \to \infty} \partial T_k/\partial v = 0 \qquad (5.7)$$

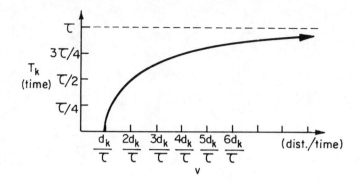

Figure 5-2. T_k versus v.

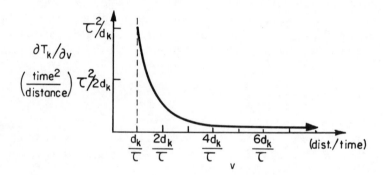

Figure 5-3. $\partial T_k / \partial v$ versus v.

Note that $\partial T_k/\partial v$ increases as d_k increases. This observation is consistent with the obvious fact that greater absolute changes in travel times result from a change in velocity where greater distances are traveled. Therefore, the more out-of-the-way a location k is relative to the shortest route between i and j, the greater the impact of a velocity change on T_k.

Figures 5-1, 5-2, and 5-3 show how changes in τ and v affect T_k in very different ways. For any point $k \in R$, the marginal changes in T_k resulting from differential changes in τ are constant (that is, independent of τ), whereas the marginal changes in T_k resulting from differential changes in v diminish as v increases. Furthermore, effects of changes in τ are independent of d_k, while effects of changes in v vary directly with d_k.

The effects of changes in τ and v on T_k can be compared in more detail by examining the elasticities of T_k with respect to these variables. An *elas-*

ticity of a dependent variable y with respect to some independent variable x is defined as

$$\eta_x^y = \frac{\partial y}{\partial x} \cdot \frac{x}{y} \tag{5.8}$$

Observe that η_x^y is a dimensionless quantity measured at a point (x, y). It can be interpreted as the percent change in y resulting from a small change in x divided by the percent change in x. Since elasticities are measures of relative sensitivities, elasticities of a dependent variable with respect to different independent variables can be compared directly. This allows comparisons to be made between the relative sensitivities of a dependent variable to changes in different independent variables.

The elasticities of T_k with respect to τ and v are

$$\eta_\tau^{T_k} = \frac{\beta_k}{\beta_k - 1} \qquad \text{for all } \tau \text{ and } v \text{ such that } \beta_k > 1 \tag{5.9}$$

and

$$\eta_v^{T_k} = \frac{1}{\beta_k - 1} \qquad \text{for all } \tau \text{ and } v \text{ such that } \beta_k > 1 \tag{5.10}$$

respectively, where

$$\beta_k = \frac{\tau}{d_k/v} \tag{5.11}$$

Observe that β_k is the ratio of the amount of time the individual has available between his coupling constraints to the minimum travel time from i to j through k.

Figure 5–4 plots $\eta_\tau^{T_k}$ versus β_k and $\eta_v^{T_k}$ versus β_k. Notice that

$$\lim_{\beta_k \to \infty} \eta_\tau^{T_k} = 1 \tag{5.12}$$

$$\lim_{\beta_k \to \infty} \eta_v^{T_k} = 0 \tag{5.13}$$

and

$$\eta_\tau^{T_k} - \eta_v^{T_k} = 1 \qquad \text{for all } \tau \text{ and } v \text{ such that } \beta_k > 1 \tag{5.14}$$

Thus the relative sensitivity of T_k resulting from a small percentage change in τ is always greater than the relative sensitivity of T_k resulting from an equal percentage change in v. Therefore, v must always be changed by a greater percent than τ in order to induce a comparable change in T_k.

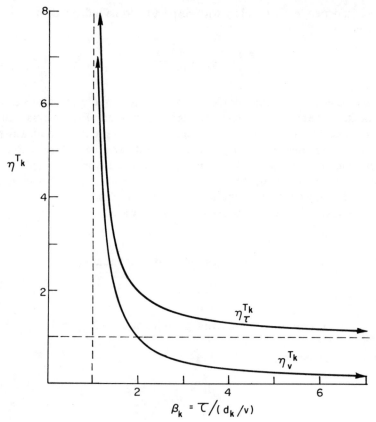

Figure 5–4. η_τ^{Tk} versus β_k and η_v^{Tk} versus β_k.

An expression for the proportional change in v required to produce a change in T_k comparable to that produced by a $\partial\tau$ change in τ is determined from the definition of an elasticity. In particular, the proportional change in T_k resulting from a $\partial\tau/\tau$ proportional change in τ is

$$\frac{\partial T_k}{T_k} = \eta_\tau^{Tk} \cdot \frac{\partial\tau}{\tau} \qquad (5.15)$$

Similarly, the proportional change in T_k resulting from a $\partial v/v$ proportional change in v is

$$\frac{\partial T_k}{T_k} = \eta_v^{Tk} \cdot \frac{\partial v}{v} \qquad (5.16)$$

Equating 5.15 and 5.16 and simplifying yields

$$\frac{\partial v}{v} = \beta_k \cdot \frac{\partial \tau}{\tau} \tag{5.17}$$

Observe that the proportional change in v required to produce the same change in T_k as a $\partial \tau$ change in τ increases linearly with β_k. Thus the less the amount of time required to travel a distance d_k relative to the amount of time available to do so, the greater the change in v required to generate a change in T_k comparable to that generated by a $\partial \tau$ change in τ.

Equation 5.17 can be rewritten as

$$\partial v = \frac{v^2}{d_k} \cdot \partial \tau \tag{5.18}$$

to provide additional insights. In particular, equation 5.18 indicates that the absolute change in v required to induce the same change in T_k as a small change in τ increases with the square of the initial velocity and the inverse of d_k. Therefore, as the individual's initial velocity increases, the change in velocity that would have the same effect on T_k as a small change in τ increases at an increasing rate. Furthermore, as the distance the individual must travel to reach k decreases, the change in velocity which would have the same effect on T_k as a small change in τ also increases at an increasing rate.

Since elasticities are defined at a point, equations 5.9, 5.10, 5.14, 5.17, and 5.18 hold only for very small changes in τ and v. Differences in the effects of larger changes in τ and v can be assessed directly from equation 5.3. Given that $v_1 > d_k / \tau_1$ and $v_1 > d_k / \tau_2$, the change in T_k produced by changing τ_1 to τ_2 is simply

$$\Delta T_k = \tau_2 - \tau_1 \tag{5.19}$$

and given that $v_2 > d_k / \tau_2$, the change in T_k produced by changing v_1 to v_2 is

$$\Delta T_k = d_k \left(\frac{1}{v_1} - \frac{1}{v_2} \right) \tag{5.20}$$

Equation 5.20 indicates the intuitive fact that the effect of a change in velocity on T_k depends on the distance d_k an individual must travel to spend time at location k.

Notice that the locations k such that

$$d_k = (\tau_2 - \tau_1)/\left(\frac{1}{v_1} - \frac{1}{v_2}\right) \tag{5.21}$$

have the same change in T_k produced by a $\tau_2 - \tau_1$ increase in τ as a $v_2 - v_1$ increase in v. Therefore, locations included in the geographical region

$$d_{ij} \leq d_k \leq (\tau_2 - \tau_1)/\left(\frac{1}{v_1} - \frac{1}{v_2}\right) \tag{5.22}$$

have greater changes in T_k produced by the increase in τ than by the increase in v. And locations k in the geographical region

$$d_k > (\tau_2 - \tau_1)/\left(\frac{1}{v_1} - \frac{1}{v_2}\right) \tag{5.23}$$

have greater changes in T_k produced by the increase in v than by the increase in τ. Observe that the latter region defined by equation 5.23 does not exist if

$$\tau_1 v_2 \leq (\tau_2 - \tau_1)/\left(\frac{1}{v_1} - \frac{1}{v_2}\right) \tag{5.24}$$

The lefthand side of equation 5.24 is the maximum distance the individual can travel and still satisfy the coupling constraints he confronts after v_1 is increased to v_2. If this distance is less than the distance that must be traveled for the velocity change to compensate for the change in τ (the righthand side of equation 5.24), then no locations can be reached such that equation 5.23 holds. The relation in equation 5.24 can be rewritten as

$$\frac{v_2 - v_1}{v_1} \leq \frac{\tau_2 - \tau_1}{\tau_1} \tag{5.25}$$

Therefore, whenever the percentage change in v is less than the percentage change in τ, the change in τ will increase the amount of time that can be spent at all reachable locations more than the change in v. This means that independent of the valuation assumptions underlying a benefit measure, the marginal benefit of a temporal strategy will always exceed the marginal benefit of a velocity strategy when these strategies and initial conditions are characterized by equation 5.25.

The two regions defined by equation 5.22 and 5.23 are depicted (with space in one dimension) in figure 5-5. In this figure, i and j correspond to

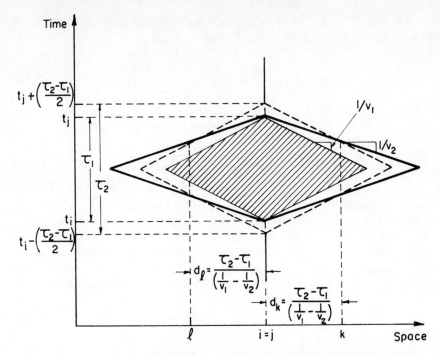

Figure 5–5. Comparison of Effects of Velocity Strategies and Temporal Strategeies on the Maximum Amount of Time that Can Be Spent at Different Locations.

the same location; the shaded portion of space–time is the original space–time prism; the prism circumscribed by heavy lines results from changing the velocity from v_1 to v_2; and the prism circumscribed with dotted lines results from changing τ_1 to τ_2. (Notice that the change in τ is spread equally between the origin time constraint and the destination time constraint.) Destinations located farther away from i than l and k comprise the region defined by equation 5.23. Destinations located closer to i than l and k comprise the region defined by equation 5.22. (Note that $d_l = d_k$.)

The existence of these two regions has important implications when one compares different velocity and temporal strategies. If locations which are not too far out of the way relative to i and j are the locations which are most attractive, then temporal strategies are more likely to have more favorable impacts than velocity strategies. If distant locations are most attractive, then velocity strategies become more favorable relative to temporal strategies. This issue is explored in greater depth in cases 2 through 6.

Changes in τ and v that produce the same change in T_k are determined by equating equations 5.19 and 5.20. Thus we have

$$v_2 - v_1 = v_1 \left[\frac{1}{1 - \dfrac{(\tau_2 - \tau_1) v_1}{d_k}} - 1 \right] \qquad (5.26)$$

or

$$\frac{v_2 - v_1}{v_1} = \frac{\tau_1 v_2}{d_k} \left(\frac{\tau_2 - \tau_1}{\tau_1} \right) \qquad (5.27)$$

Notice that equation 5.27 approaches equation 5.17 when $v_2 - v_1$ and $\tau_2 - \tau_1$ become very small. Furthermore, $v_2 - v_1$ varies with the difference in τ independent of the size of τ and depends on v_1. Therefore, the greater the initial velocity v_1, the greater must be the increase in velocity to produce the same change in T_k as a $\tau_2 - \tau_1$ change in τ_1. Finally, as $\tau_2 - \tau_1$ approaches d_k / v_1, the comparable increase in velocity approaches infinity, that is,

$$\lim_{(\tau_2 - \tau_1) \to d_k / v_1} (v_2 - v_1) = \infty \qquad (5.28)$$

This results because the amount of time that can be spent at location k equals τ_1, the initial amount of time the individual has available, when

$$\tau_2 - \tau_1 = d_k / v_1 \qquad (5.29)$$

And if τ_1 and d_k remain fixed, the individual would have to be able to travel the distance d_k without consuming any time for T_k to equal τ_1. The only way this could happen is if $v_2 - v_1$ approached infinity.

Figures 5–6 and 5–7 provide examples of changes in τ and v which provide equivalent changes in T_k. Figure 5–6 plots $v_2 - v_1$ versus $\tau_2 - \tau_1$ for $v_1 = 20$ mi/h and different values of d_k. Figure 5–7 plots $v_2 - v_1$ versus $\tau_2 - \tau_1$ for $d_k = 10$ mi and different values of v_1.

In summary, this case highlights the essential difference between the effects of velocity strategies and temporal strategies on the maximum amounts of time individuals can spend at different locations T_k. In particular, it illustrates the following:

1. The effect on T_k of a given velocity change diminishes at an increasing rate as an individual's initial velocity v increases and as the distance d_k from an individual's origin to his final destination through the location k decreases.

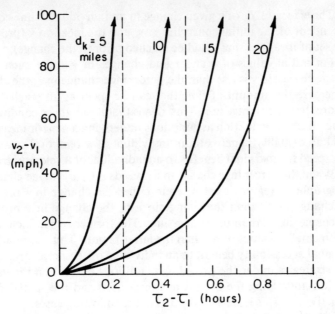

Figure 5–6. $v_2 - v_1$ versus $\tau_2 - \tau_1$ for $v_1 = 20$ mi/h.

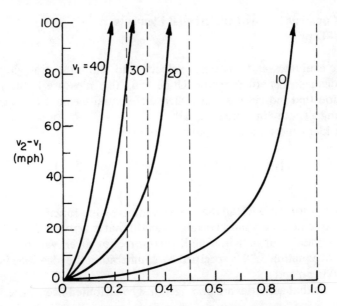

Figure 5–7. $v_2 - v_1$ versus $\tau_2 - \tau_1$ for $d_k = 10$ miles.

2. The effect on T_k of a given change in an individual's time constraint is independent of the initial constraint τ, v, and the location k (providing k is in the set of locations that could be reached prior to the change).

3. For initial values of v and τ and changes in v and τ such that the percentage change in v is less than the percentage change in τ, the change in τ will increase the amount of time that can be spent at all reachable locations more than the change in v. This means that under these conditions and independent of the valuation assumptions underlying a benefit measure, the marginal accessibility benefits to an individual of a temporal strategy will always exceed the marginal benefits to an individual of a velocity strategy.

4. When the percentage change in v exceeds the percentage change in τ, two geographical regions exist wherein either the change in τ produced a greater change in T_k than the change in v or the change in v produced a greater change in T_k than the change in τ. The former region includes locations with smaller values of d_k than the latter region. Thus comparisons of the marginal accessibility benefit to an individual of temporal strategies and velocity strategies under the preceding conditions depend on the valuation assumption underlying the benefit measures used and the spatial distribution of activities. This issue is illustrated in the following cases.

Case 2: Constant Value of Differential Elements of Space-Time

This case evaluates and compares velocity and temporal strategies with a simple idealized benefit measure. Underlying this measure is the implicit assumption that individuals value each differential element of space-time comprising a space-time prism equally.

Consider benefit measures having the form

$$f[(d_k, a_k, T_k)_{k \in R}] = \sum_{k \in R} q(d_k) \cdot a_k \cdot u(T_k) \tag{5.30}$$

(This is equation 4.8.) Recall that q is a nonincreasing function that is unity for $d_k = 0$, and u is a nondecreasing function that is zero for $T_k = 0$. For a given distribution of activities and, therefore, for given values of a_k, the measure in equation 5.30 is specified by enumerating the locations in R and by specifying q and u.

Assume that activities are homogenously distributed over space, that is,

$$a_k = a \qquad \text{for all } k \in R \tag{5.31}$$

Furthermore, consider

$$q(d_k) = 1 \qquad \text{for all } k \in R \tag{5.32}$$

Here, q is specified so that the value of an opportunity is not discounted with distance (except in the sense that distance affects T_k). This is analogous to the role of distance in the spatial–accessibility measure proposed in Wachs and Kumagai.[1] Equation 5.30 becomes

$$f[(d_k, a_k, T_k)_{k \in R}] = a \sum_{k \in R} u(T_k) \tag{5.33}$$

Since the distribution of the values of a_k is assumed to be smooth, locations can now be specified continuously over space rather than discretely. In particular, a location k can be represented in terms of its x and y components and the righthand side of equation 5.33 can be rewritten as

$$a \sum_{k \in R} u(T_k) = a \iint_{(x,y) \in R} u(T_{xy}) \, dx \, dy \tag{5.34}$$

where

$$T_{xy} = \begin{cases} \tau - d_{xy}/v & \text{for all } (x, y) \in R \\ 0 & \text{otherwise} \end{cases} \tag{5.35}$$

and the distance d_{xy} is defined analogous to d_k.

In this continuous specification, represent the origin location i as (x_i, y_i) and the destination location j as (x_j, y_j). Also, denote d as the distance between (x_i, y_i) and (x_j, y_j).

The distances d_{xy} and d depend on the network the individual is restricted to travel on. This case makes the extreme assumption that the individual can travel in all directions. Therefore,

$$d_{xy} = [(x - x_i)^2 + (y - y_i)^2]^{1/2} + [(x_j - x)^2 + (y_j - y)^2]^{1/2}$$

and

$$d = [(x_j - x_i)^2 + (y_j - y_i)^2]^{1/2} \tag{5.36}$$

Under this assumption, the geographical region R encompassing the locations the individual can reach and still satisfy the coupling constraints that he confronts is bounded by an ellipse with foci at (x_i, y_i) and (x_j, y_j). The equation of this ellipse is

$$\tau = d_{xy}/v \tag{5.37}$$

A closed–form expression for the righthand side of equation 5.34 can be developed by specifying u. In this case, consider

$$u(T_{xy}) = cT_{xy} \qquad (5.38)$$

where c = a scale parameter.

The benefit measure specified according to the assumption made here becomes

$$a \iint_{(x,y)\in R} u(T_{xy}) \, dxdy = b \iint_{(x,y)\in R} T_{xy} \, dxdy \qquad (5.39)$$

where $b = ca$.

Simplifying equation 5.39 gives

$$BM_2 = \frac{b\pi}{12} v^2 [\tau^2 - (\frac{d}{v})^2]^{3/2} \qquad (5.40)$$

where BM_2 represents the benefit measure developed in this case.

Underlying equation 5.40 are assumptions about the value an individual derives from an opportunity. Here, activity levels are assumed to be homogeneous, and opportunity values are not discounted with distance, that is, $q(d_k) = 1$. Therefore, the values of opportunities are distinguished only by the amount of time that can be spent at the location of an opportunity. And since u is specified such that each unit of time is weighted the same, equation 5.40 implicitly assumes that each differential element of space–time ($dxdydt$) is valued the same (independent of the location of the opportunity and the amount of time that can be spent there.

BM_2 without the scale parameter b is the same as a measure of the "volume" of a behavioral space proposed by Lenntorp.[2] Observe that BM_2 depends only on τ, v, d, and the scale parameter b. Since b in part depends on the units that τ, v, and d are measured in, BM_2 has no meaning as an absolute measure of benefit. This is not a problem here, however, since interest lies in comparing the marginal benefits of strategies affecting τ and v. And, as illustrated later, these comparisons can be made independent of b.

The relative sensitivities of BM_2 with respect to τ and v are initially evaluated and compared in terms of the elasticity of BM_2 with respect to these variables. Recall the definition of an elasticity in equation 5.8 and the subsequent interpretation of this measure of sensitivity.

The elasticities of interest here are defined as

$$\eta_\tau^{BM_2} = \frac{3\beta^2}{\beta^2 - 1} \quad \text{for all } \beta > 1 \tag{5.41}$$

and

$$\eta_v^{BM_2} = \frac{3}{\beta^2 - 1} + 2 \quad \text{for all } \beta > 1 \tag{5.42}$$

where

$$\beta = \frac{\tau}{d/v} = \frac{v}{d/\tau} = \frac{\tau v}{d} \tag{5.43}$$

Notice that the value of β is equivalent to the ratio of:

1. The amount of time the individual has available (τ) to the minimum travel time from the individual's origin (x_i, y_i) to his or her final destination (x_j, y_j), (d/v).
2. The individual's maximum velocity (v) to the velocity which would just allow the individual to satisfy his coupling constraints (d/τ).
3. The maximum distance the individual could travel (τv) to the distance he must travel (d).

In essence, β is a measure of the degree to which an individual's coupling constraints are binding. As β approaches unity, the individual has just barely enough time available to travel the required distance. If β is much greater than 1, the minimum amount of time spent traveling only slightly impinges on the amount of time the individual has available.

Observe that

$$\eta_\tau^{BM_2} - \eta_v^{BM_2} = 1 \quad \text{for all } \beta > 1 \tag{5.44}$$

$$\lim_{\beta \to \infty} \eta_\tau^{BM_2} = 3 \tag{5.45}$$

$$\lim_{\beta \to \infty} \eta_v^{BM_2} = 2 \tag{5.46}$$

$$\lim_{\beta \to 1} \eta_\tau^{BM^2} = \infty \tag{5.47}$$

and

$$\lim_{\beta \to 1} \eta_v^{BM^2} = \infty \tag{5.48}$$

Therefore, the relative sensitivity of BM_2 with respect to τ is always greater than the relative sensitivity of BM_2 with respect to v. Furthermore, as the coupling constraints become less binding, the relative sensitivities of BM_2 with respect to τ and v both approach constants. Moreover, as the coupling constraints become more binding, the relative sensitivities of BM_2 with re-

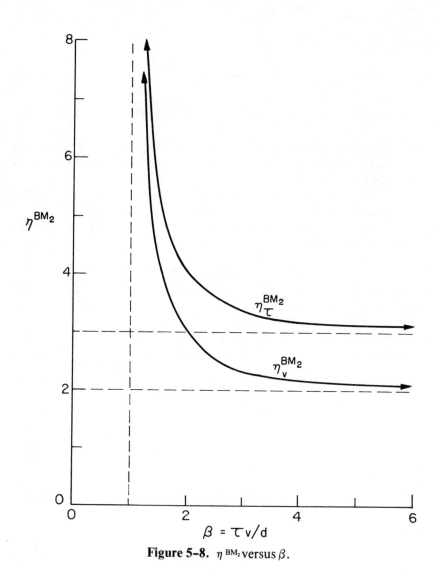

Figure 5–8. η^{BM_2} versus β.

spect to τ and v become very large. These results are depicted in figure 5.8 where $\eta_\tau^{BM_2}$ versus β and $\eta_v^{BM_2}$ versus β are both plotted.

Observe from figures 5–8 that strategies which influence β (by changing τ, v, and/or d) will have much greater *relative* impacts on individuals confronted with coupling constraints which are quite binding, than upon individuals confronted with coupling constraints which are not so binding. The greater relative change in BM_2 resulting when β is small does not imply that the marginal benefits to an individual of these relative changes decrease with β. Since BM_2 results from assuming that each differential element of space–time available to an individual is valued equally, the marginal benefit implications of some relative change in BM_2 depend on the corresponding absolute change in BM_2. It can be demonstrated that as β increases, the absolute sensitivity of BM_2 to changes in τ and v increases. Thus, under the valuation assumptions made here, individuals in more flexible situations benefit more in an absolute sense from increases in τ and v than individuals who are more constrained. This is a direct result of the fact that BM_2 is developed by assuming that the values of opportunities are not discounted with distance and that these values increase at a constant rate with increases in the amount of time that can be spent at locations.

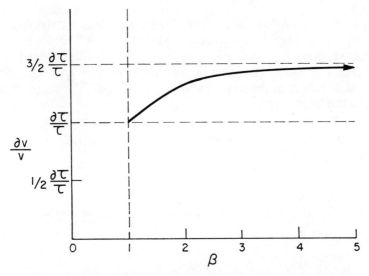

Figure 5-9. $\dfrac{\partial v}{v}$ versus β for Fixed Percentage Change in τ.

An expression for the proportional change in v required to produce the same marginal benefits as a $\partial\tau$ change in τ can be determined from the definition of an elasticity. Let

$$\frac{\partial v}{v} = \frac{\eta_\tau^{BM_2}}{\eta_v^{BM_2}} \cdot \frac{\partial\tau}{\tau} \qquad (5.49)$$

or

$$\frac{\partial v}{v} = \left(\frac{3\beta^2}{2\beta^2 + 1}\right)\frac{\partial\tau}{\tau} \qquad \text{for all } \beta > 1 \qquad (5.50)$$

Observe that when $\beta = 1$, $\dfrac{\partial v}{v} = \dfrac{\partial\tau}{\tau}$, and as β becomes very large, $\dfrac{\partial v}{v} \to \dfrac{3}{2}\dfrac{\partial\tau}{\tau}$. This change is depicted in figure 5–9, where $\dfrac{\partial v}{v}$ versus β is plotted for a fixed–percentage change in τ.

Equation 5.50 indicates that a greater proportional change in v is always required to produce the same marginal benefit as a $\partial\tau$ change in τ. Furthermore, this comparable proportional change in v increases as the the coupling constraints an individual confronts become less binding There-fore, in the context of BM_2, the more constraining the situation, the more closely a velocity strategy approaches the attractiveness of a temporal strategy.

Equations 5.44, 5.49, and 5.50 and the conclusions derived from these equations hold only for small changes in τ and v. Differences in changes in benefits resulting from larger changes in τ and v can be assessed directly from equation 5.40. Consider an initial value of τ and v, denoted τ_1 and v_1, and assume that τ_1 increases to τ_2 and v remains fixed. The change in bene-fit from this increase in τ is

$$\Delta BM_2^\tau = c\left[\frac{(\tau_2^2 v_1^2 - d^2)^{3/2}}{v_1} - \frac{(\tau_1^2 v_1^2 - d^2)^{3/2}}{v_1}\right] \qquad (5.51)$$

where $c = \dfrac{b\pi}{12}$. Now assume that v_1 increases to v_2 while τ remains fixed. The change in benefit from this increase in v is

$$\Delta BM_2^v = c\left[\frac{(\tau_1^2 v_2^2 - d^2)^{3/2}}{v_2} - \frac{(\tau_1^2 v_1^2 - d^2)^{3/2}}{v_1}\right] \qquad (5.52)$$

Equation 5.51 and 5.52 provides an expression for determining the values of

τ_1, τ_2, v_1, and v_2 that result in an equivalent change in benefits. Thus we have

$$\frac{\tau_2}{\tau_1} = \left[\left(\frac{v_2}{v_1}\right)^{4/3} + \frac{1}{\beta^2} - \frac{1}{\beta^2 \left(\frac{v_2}{v_1}\right)^{2/3}} \right]^{1/2} \qquad (5.53)$$

Figure 5–10 plots τ_2/τ_1 versus v_2/v_1 for different values of β. Observe that (1) v_2/v_1 is always greater than τ_2/τ_1 whenever $v_2 > v_1$, (2) the difference between τ_2/τ_1 and v_2/v_1 increases at a decreasing rate as β increases, and (3) τ_2/τ_1 increases at a decreasing rate with v_2/v_1. These observations are consistent with those made from examining the elasticities of BM_2 with respect to v and τ.

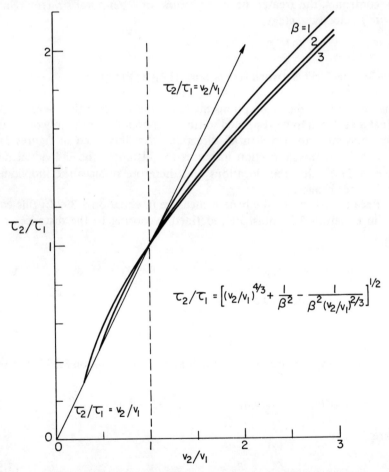

Figure 5–10. τ_2/τ_1 versus v_2/v_1 for Different Values of β.

In summary this case develops a measure of benefit which implicitly assumes that an individual places equal value on each differential element of space-time comprising a space-time prism. The space-time prism for which this measure is developed corresponds to the case in which an individual can travel in all directions.

Using the measure developed here, conclusions follow regarding the marginal benefits to an individual of velocity strategies versus temporal strategies:

1. To produce the same marginal benefit as a given change in τ, v must always be changed by a greater proportion than τ.
2. The less constrained an individual is by the coupling constraints he confronts, the greater the attractiveness of a temporal strategy relative to a velocity strategy.

Case 3: Fine–Grid Network versus Travel in All Directions

This case follows the assumptions made in case 2 except that here an individual is assumed to be restricted to traveling on a fine–grid network rather than being able to travel in all directions. As illustrated in figures 3–11 through 3–14, this restriction increases the distances the individual must travel to reach different locations and therefore reduces the individual's space–time autonomy.

Recall the form of the benefit measure in equation 5.39. In this case, T_{xy} in equation 5.39 must be redefined according to the distances d_{xy}, where

$$d_{xy} = |x - x_i| + |x_j - x| + |y - y_i| + |y_j - y| \quad (5.54)$$

Also, d must be redefined as

$$d = |x_j - x_i| + |y_j - y_i| \quad (5.55)$$

Under these conditions, the benefit measure in equation 5.39 becomes

$$\text{BM}_3 = b\left[(\tau - d/v)\partial_x\partial_y + \frac{(\tau - d/v)^2}{2}vd + \frac{(\tau - d/v)^3}{6}v^2 \right] \quad (5.56)$$

where

$$\partial_x = |x_j - x_i| \quad (5.57)$$

and

$$\partial_y = | \, y_j - y_i \, | \qquad (5.58)$$

Notice that in addition to BM_3 depending on τ, v, d, and b, it also depends on the product of the x and y components of d. This product is a maximum when these components are equal and is zero if one of the components is zero. Therefore, benefits (as measured here) are greatest when coupling constraints are located such that the distance between them consists of equal x and y components and least when coupling constraints are located on the same link (that is, either the x or y component is zero). This suggests that a circular city is more likely to provide greater accessibility than a linear city when activities are homogenously distributed.

As was the case with BM_2, it can be shown that

$$\eta_{\dot{v}}^{BM_3} - \eta_{\dot{\tau}}^{BM_3} = 1 \qquad (5.59)$$

and therefore, a greater proportional change in v is always required to produce the same marginal benefit as a $\partial\tau$ change in τ. Furthermore, it can be demonstrated that the results obtained in case 2 regarding the comparability of velocity strategies and temporal strategies also hold in this case.

The effect of restricting travel to a fine–grid network on the benefits an individual derives from his space–time autonomy is of interest here. These effects are assessed as follows.

Consider destination coupling constraints distributed on a circle of radius d. If an individual can travel in all directions, the benefits of the space–time autonomy corresponding to each destination on this circle are the same and are expressed as BM_2 in equation 5.40. However, if the individual is restricted to traveling on a fine grid, the benefits of the space–time autonomy corresponding to each destination on the circle depend on the precise location of the destination. These benefits are defined by

$$BM_3 = b \left[\frac{\tau^3 v^2}{6} + \frac{\tau d^2}{2} + \frac{d^2(\cos^3 \zeta + \sin^3 \zeta)}{3v} \right] \qquad (5.60)$$

where

$$\partial_x = d \cos \zeta \qquad (5.61)$$

and

$$\partial_y = d \sin \zeta \qquad (5.62)$$

are the x and y components of the distance to the point (d, ζ) when the grid is followed. The average value over the circle of BM_3 is

$$\overline{BM}_3 = b \left(\frac{\tau^3 v^2}{6} - \frac{\tau d^2}{2} + \frac{8}{9\pi} \frac{d^3}{v} \right) \qquad (5.63)$$

Figure 5-11 plots the percentage difference between BM_2 and $\overline{BM}_3$ versus β. Observe that (1) the effect of restricting travel to find a grid decreases as the coupling constraints an individual confronts become less binding, and (2) the percentage difference between BM_2 and $\overline{BM}_3$ asymptotically approaches $(1 - \frac{2}{\pi}) \times 100\% = 36.3\%$ as β becomes very large. Therefore, restricting travel to a fine grid will, at a minimum, reduce the benefits of an individual's space–time autonomy by 36.3 percent.

In summary, case 3 is the same as case 2 except that an individual is assumed here to be restricted to traveling on a fine–grid network rather than being able to travel in all directions. Under this condition and using a benefit measure that implicitly assumes that individuals value each differential element of space–time equally, the results regarding temporal and velocity strategies summarized at the end of case 2 hold. Furthermore, this case suggests the following:

1. A circular city is more likely to provide greater accessibility than a linear city when activities are homogenously distributed and the network is a fine grid.
2. The effect of restricting travel to a fine grid decreases as the coupling constraints an individual confronts become less binding and will reduce benefits of an individual's space–time autonomy by a minimum of 36.3 percent.

Case 4: General Specification of the Marginal Value of Time Available at Locations

The benefit measures developed and applied in cases 2 and 3 result from assuming that the marginal value of the maximum amount of time an individual can spend at a location is constant. This means that an additional minute available at a location is assumed to be valued the same by an individual independent of the amount of time that can already be spent there. Here, this assumption is relaxed by introducing a more general specification of the function u in equation 5.34. This specification allows comparisons of temporal and velocity strategies under a broader range of assumptions regarding an individual's valuations of opportunities.

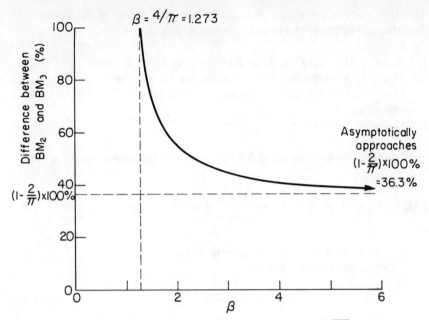

Figure 5-11. Percentage Difference betweem BM_2 and $\overline{BM}_3$ versus β.

The benefit measure developed here has the form specified in equation 5.34. Recall that measures having this form do not discount the value individuals derive from an opportunity with distance except in the sense that distance affects T_{xy} . Such measures also assume that activities are homogenously distributed.

In this case, individuals are assumed to be restricted to traveling on a fine-grid network. Thus distances and T_{xy} are defined as in case 3.

A closed-form expression for measures characterized by equation 5.34 is developed by specifying the function u in this equation. Consider the case in which

$$u(T_{xy}) = (cT_{xy})^{\alpha} \qquad \text{for all } \alpha \geq 0 \qquad (5.64)$$

Observe that

1. u is nondecreasing.
2. $u(0) = 0$ (except where $\alpha = 0$).
3. The specification of u in cases 2 and 3 is attained when $\alpha = 1$.
4.
$$\frac{du(T_{xy})}{dT_{xy}} = \alpha KT_{xy}^{\alpha-1} \quad \text{where } K = c^{\alpha} \qquad (5.65)$$

This last observation indicates that the marginal value of the amount of time that can be spent at a location depends on α. Therefore,

1. If $\alpha < 1$, this marginal value diminishes as T_{xy} increases.
2. If $\alpha > 1$, this marginal value increases as T_{xy} increases.
3. If $\alpha = 1$, this marginal value remains constant as T_{xy} increases (as in cases 2 and 3).
4. If $\alpha = 0$, this marginal value is zero.

Specifying u as in equation 5.64 provides the following benefit measure:

$$\text{BM}_4 = K \left[(\tau - d/v)^\alpha \partial_x \partial_y + \frac{(\tau - d/v)^{\alpha+1} vd}{\alpha + 1} + \frac{(\tau - d/v)^{\alpha+2} v^2}{(\alpha + 1)(\alpha + 2)} \right] \quad (5.66)$$

Notice that when $\alpha = 1$, BM_4 reduces to BM_3.
   It can be demonstrated that

$$\eta_\tau^{\text{BM}_4} - \eta_v^{\text{BM}_4} = \alpha \quad (5.67)$$

for all values of τ, v, and d such that $\tau v/d > 1$. Since $\alpha \geq 0$, results regarding temporal and velocity strategies developed in case 2 hold in this case (except $\alpha = 0$). However, now the attractiveness of a change in velocity relative to a change in τ depends on α. When $\alpha < 1$, a given change in v becomes more attractive relative to a given change in τ. When $\alpha > 1$ the velocity strategy becomes less attractive relative to the given temporal strategy. This results from the fact that velocity strategies have greater impacts on distant locations than on proximate locations and the amounts of time that can be spent at distant locations is less than the amounts of time that can be spent at proximate locations.
   By letting $d = 0$ in equation 5.65, the effect of different values of α on the relative attractiveness of temporal and velocity strategies can be illustrated. In particular, when $d = 0$,

$$\text{BM}_4 = \frac{K \tau^{\alpha+2} v^2}{(\alpha + 1)(\alpha + 2)} \quad (5.68)$$

Now consider an initial value of τ and v, denoted as τ_1 and v_1, and assume that in one case, τ_1 increases to τ_2 and v remains fixed, and in another case, v_1 increases to v_2 and τ remains fixed. In order for the change in v to induce a comparable change in BM_4 as the change in τ, the following must hold:

$$\frac{K\tau_2^{\alpha+2} v_1^2}{(\alpha + 1)(\alpha + 2)} = \frac{K\tau_1^{\alpha+2} v_2^2}{(\alpha + 1)(\alpha + 2)} \qquad (5.69)$$

This simplifies to

$$\epsilon_v = (1 + \epsilon_\tau)^{(\alpha+2)/2} - 1 \qquad (5.70)$$

where

$$\epsilon_\tau = \frac{\tau_2 - \tau_1}{\tau_1} \qquad (5.71)$$

and

$$\epsilon_v = \frac{v_2 - v_1}{v_1} \qquad (5.72)$$

Figure 5-12 plots ϵ_v versus ϵ_τ for different values of α. Observe that when $\alpha = 0$, $\epsilon_v = \epsilon_\tau$, and as α increases, v must change by an increasingly greater percent than τ to generate a comparable change in BM_4.

When $\alpha = 0$, $u(T_{xy}) = 1$ independent of T_{xy}, and from a marginal benefit standpoint, temporal and velocity strategies are viewed as having the same effects. This is analogous to assuming no distance discounting, that is, $q(d_{xy}) = 1$ for all d_{xy}.

The case where $\alpha = 0$ provides interesting insights between the benefit measures proposed in this study and conventional spatial–accessibility measures. Weibull[3] demonstrates that most spatial–accessibility measures in use today have the general form

$$f[(d_k, a_k)_{k=1}^n] = \sum_{k=1}^n a_k \cdot q(d_k) \qquad (5.73)$$

This is the exact form of the benefit measure proposed here when $\alpha = 0$. Consequently, conventional spatial–accessibility measures are special cases of the more general benefit measures proposed here.

In summary, case 4 develops benefit measures with a general specification of the dependence of the value an individual derives from an opportunity on the amount of time that can be spent at an opportunity. It is demonstrated that independent of whether an individual values an opportunity relative to T_{xy} with decreasing, constant, or increasing marginal value, the results regarding temporal and velocity strategies developed in case

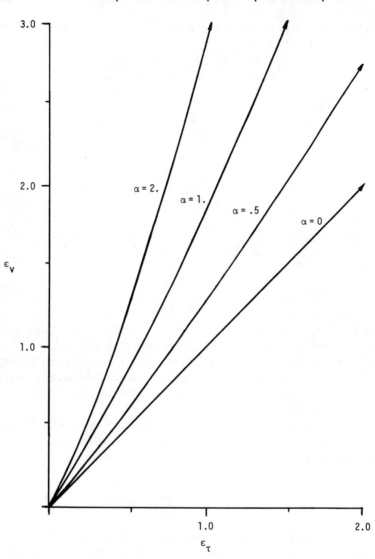

Figure 5–12. ϵ_v versus ϵ_τ for Different Values of α.

2 hold. Furthermore, the relative attractiveness of a given velocity strategy to a given temporal strategy depends on the assumed marginal value of T_{xy}. The faster this marginal value decreases as T_{xy} increases, the more attractive the velocity strategy becomes relative to the temporal strategy. Finally, conventional accessibility measures in use today are shown to be special cases of the measures developed in this case.

Case 5: Distance Discounting

The previous cases assume that distance affects the value of an opportunity only in terms of the manner in which it affects the amount of time that can be spent at the location of the opportunity. Because, among other things, the monetary cost of travel increases with distance, the value of an opportunity most likely decreases with distance. That is, for $d_1 > d_2$, $z(d_1, a, T) < z(d_2, a, T)$.

Benefit measures can be discounted by distance through specification of the function q in equation 5.30 of case 2. An example of such a function is

$$q(d_k) = \exp(-\omega d_k) \tag{5.74}$$

Observe that $q(0) = 1$ and

$$\lim_{d_k \to \infty} q(d_k) = 0 \tag{5.75}$$

Also observe that as ω increases, the degree of distance discounting increases. Function 5.74 is a common specification of a distance–discounting function used in gravity models.[4]

Since velocity strategies have more favorable impacts on the value of opportunities that are farther away, incorporating a distance–discounting function in equation 5.30 will result in velocity strategies being less attractive than in cases 2 through 4. Thus even greater velocity increases are required to increase benefits the same amount as some increase in τ when distances are assumed to affect benefit measures as in equation 5.74. To illustrate this result, replace equation 5.32 in case 2 with equation 5.74. This provides benefit measures with the form

$$f[(d_k, a_k, T_k)] = a \sum_{k \in R} u(T_k) \cdot \exp(-\omega d_k) \tag{5.76}$$

Specifying locations continuously over space, assuming a network that allows travel in all directions, and assuming the origin location (x_i, y_i) and the destination location (x_j, y_j) are the same (that is, $d = 0$), equation 5.36 gives

$$\text{BM}_5 = a \iint_{(x,y) \in R} u(T_{xy}) \cdot \exp(-\omega d_{xy}) \, dx \, dy \tag{5.77}$$

where T_{xy} is defined as in equation 5.35 and d_{xy} is defined as in equation 5.36. Finally, specifying u such that

$$u(T_{xy}) = cT_{xy} \tag{5.78}$$

(that is, assuming constant marginal utility of the amount of time available at locations) and simplifying yields

$$BM_5 = C\left[\frac{\tau}{4\omega^2} - \frac{1}{2\omega^3} + \exp(-\omega\tau v)(\frac{\tau}{4\omega^2} + \frac{1}{2\omega^3 v}) \right] \qquad (5.79)$$

where

$$C = 2\pi ac \qquad (5.80)$$

As in cases 2 and 3, it can be shown that

$$\eta_\tau^{BM_5} - \eta_v^{BM_5} = 1 \qquad (5.81)$$

and therefore, a greater proportional change in v is always required to produce the same marginal benefit as a $\partial\tau$ change in τ.

The comparability of velocity strategies and temporal strategies can be assessed in this case by recalling the expression in equation 5.49 that defines the proportional change in v required to produce the same marginal benefit as a $\partial\tau$ change in τ. Specifically,

$$\frac{\partial v}{v} = \frac{\eta_\tau^{BM_5}}{\eta_v^{BM_5}} \cdot \frac{\partial\tau}{\tau} \qquad (5.82)$$

or

$$\frac{\partial v}{v} = \frac{[\gamma - \exp(-\gamma) \cdot (\gamma^2 + \gamma)]}{[2 - \exp(-\gamma) \cdot (\gamma^2 + 2\gamma + 2)]} \cdot \frac{\partial\tau}{\tau} \qquad (5.83)$$

where

$$\gamma = \omega\tau v \qquad (5.84)$$

Figure 5–13 plots $\partial v/v$ versus γ for a fixed percentage change in τ. Observe that as $\omega \to 0$, $\gamma \to 0$ and

$$\frac{\partial v}{v} \to \frac{3}{2}\frac{\partial\tau}{\tau} \qquad (5.85)$$

This is identical to the result obtained when $\beta \to \infty$ in equation 5.50. This follows from the fact that when $d = 0$, $\beta \to \infty$. Also, observe that as $\gamma \to \infty$,

$$\frac{\partial v}{v} \to \frac{\gamma}{2} \cdot \frac{\partial\tau}{\tau} \qquad (5.86)$$

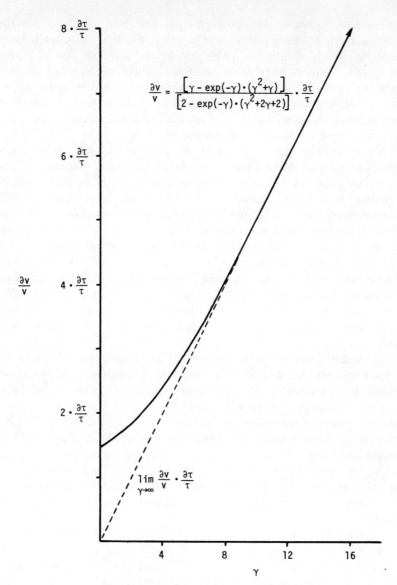

$$\frac{\partial v}{v} = \frac{\left[\gamma - \exp(-\gamma)\cdot(\gamma^2+\gamma)\right]}{\left[2 - \exp(-\gamma)\cdot(\gamma^2+2\gamma+2)\right]} \cdot \frac{\partial \tau}{\tau}$$

Figure 5-13. $\partial v/v$ versus γ for Fixed $\partial \tau/\tau$.

It is clear from figure 5-13 that as γ increases, v must increase by an increasingly greater amount to induce a marginal benefit comparable to that resulting from a $\partial \tau$ change in τ. Thus, as γ becomes larger, the attractiveness of a given velocity strategy *relative* to a given temporal strategy diminishes. Observe that γ increases with increasing τ, v, and ω. Therefore, for a given level of distance discounting (that is, for fixed ω), the larger the individual's original time budget and velocity, the less attractive a given velocity increase is *relative* to a given time budget increase. Moreover, for fixed τ and v, the more distance is discounted (that is, the larger ω), the less attractive a given velocity increase is *relative* to a given time budget increase.

This first observation is consistent with results obtained in previous cases regarding the comparability of temporal and velocity strategies. The latter observation warrants further discussion.

As suggested earlier, the value of an opportunity decreases with distance in part because the monetary cost of travel increases with distance. In this context, ω can be interpreted as the extent to which the monetary cost of travel serves as a barrier to interaction. Consistent with the notion of diminishing marginal utility of income in microeconomic consumer theory, one can therefore argue that ω decreases as income increases; that is, the monetary cost of travel becomes less of barrier to interaction as an individual's income increases. This observation, in conjuction with the results presented in figure 5-13, leads one to conclude that given a low-income individual and a high-income individual with the *same* initial time budget and velocity, the attractiveness of a given velocity strategy *relative* to a given temporal strategy will be less for the low-income person than the high-income person.

A conclusion pertaining to the accessibility implication of increasing fuel prices can also be obtained from this case. In particular, as fuel prices increase, ω will increase (that is, distance is discounted more), and therefore, a given velocity strategy will become less attractive *relative* to a given temporal strategy. Thus, in an energy-scarce world, it becomes even more important to allow individuals to recognize accessibility gains through temporal strategies.

It can be shown that the qualitative conclusions reached in this case also apply when the assumptions that (1) individuals are capable of traveling in all directions and (2) the origin and destination locations are the same are relaxed.

In summary, case 5 recognizes that the value of an opportunity will decrease with distance for reasons other than the fact that distance affects the amount of time that can be spent at the location of an opportunity. In particular, it recognizes that the monetary cost of travel increases with distance and, therefore, that the value of an opportunity should be further discounted by distance.

Using a distance-discounting function analogous to one used in gravity models, benefit measures incorporating distance discounting are developed. An analysis of these measures yields the following conclusions:

1. Since velocity strategies have more favorable impacts on the value of opportunities that are farther away, distance discounting results in a decline in the attractiveness of velocity strategies *relative* to temporal strategies.

The greater the degree of distance discounting, the greater the decline in the relative attractiveness of velocity strategies.

2. For a given level of distance discounting, the larger an individual's original time budget and velocity, the less attractive a given velocity strategy is relative to a given temporal strategy.

3. Given a low-income individual and a high-income individual with the same initial time budget and velocity, the attractiveness of a given velocity strategy relative to a given temporal strategy will be less for the low-income individual than the high-income individual.

4. As fuel prices increase, the degree of distance discounting will increase, and as a result, a given velocity strategy will become less attractive *relative* to a given temporal strategy. Therefore, in an energy-scarce world, it becomes even more important for individuals to recognize accessibility gains through temporal strategies.

Case 6: Alternative-Activity Distributions

The previous cases assume that activities are distributed homogenously over geographical space. But in reality, activity distributions are characterized by peaks and valleys. Clearly, if the most attractive activities are at locations in close proximity, the relative advantage of a temporal strategy over a velocity strategy increases. Moreover, if attractive activities are at out-of-the-way locations, velocity strategies increase in importance. Therefore, land-use policies and other strategies that increase the density of activities will increase the attractiveness of temporal strategies. Policies that encourage urban sprawl increase the importance of velocity strategies.

As discussed in the summary of case 1, independent of the distribution of activities, if v is changed by a less percentage than τ, the corresponding temporal strategy will always increase benefits more than the corresponding velocity strategy. When v is increased by a greater percentage, the strategy generating the greatest marginal benefit depends on the activity distribution.

The effects of different activity distributions can be examined by developing idealized distributions of the values of a_k which vary smoothly with d_k. This is accomplished here in the context of an individual confronted with

1. An origin coupling constraint and a destination coupling constraint having the same geographical location (0,0)
2. A time budget τ,
3. A mode that is available at all times and operates at a constant maximum velocity v on a fine-grid network

Here the individual must return to his original location after a given period of time τ. This assumption is made for simplicity and does not detract from the essence of the problem being addressed in this case. Furthermore, specifying the origin location to be (0,0) is done without any loss of generality. The locations the individual can reach and still satisfy the coupling constraints he confronts are encompassed in the region R, depicted in Figure 5–14.

Consider a total level of acitivity A distributed over R. Let $\varrho(x, y)$ equal the density of activities at location (x, y). Observe that

$$A = \iint\limits_R \varrho(x, y)\,dxdy \qquad (5.87)$$

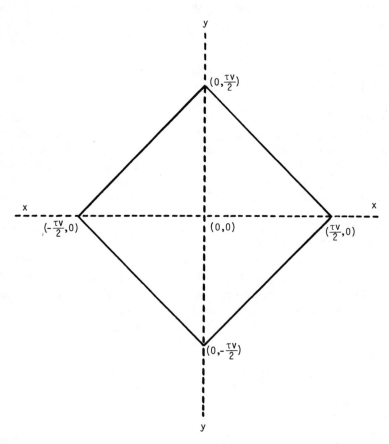

Figure 5–14. Geographical Region R Encompassing the Locations an Individual Can Reach Given a Time Constraint τ and the Ability to Travel at a Velocity v on a Fine–Grid Network.

The objective here is to compare the accessibility of the individual for different activity distributions (that is, different specifications of $\varrho(x, y)$ in equation 5.87). Initially, activity distributions characterized by densities that very linearly with distance from the individual's origin (0,0) and satisfy equation 5.88 are considered. In particular, let

$$\varrho(x, y) = \varrho_0 + \lambda(|x| + |y|) \qquad \text{for } \lambda > 0 \text{ and } \varrho_0 \geq 0 \qquad (5.88)$$

and

$$\varrho(x, y) = \begin{cases} \varrho_0 + \lambda(|x| + |y|) & \text{for } \lambda < 0 \text{ and } |x| + |y| \leq \dfrac{\varrho_0}{|\lambda|} \\ 0 & \text{otherwise} \end{cases} \qquad (5.89)$$

where ϱ_0 = the density of activities at (0,0)
λ = the rate at which the density of activities changes with respect to the distance from location (0,0).

Observe that

1. If $\lambda = 0$, the activity distribution is homogenous.
2. If $\lambda > 0$, the density of activities increases with distance from location (0,0).
3. If $\lambda < 0$, the density of activities decreases with distance from location (0,0).

Also observe that for the condition 5.87 to hold, ϱ_0 and λ must be specified such that

$$A = \varrho_0 \frac{\tau^2 v^2}{2} + \frac{\lambda \tau^3 v^3}{6} \qquad (5.90)$$

or

$$\varrho_0 = \frac{2A}{\tau^3 v^2} - \frac{\lambda \tau v}{3} \qquad (5.91)$$

Equation 5.91 applies for $-12A/(\tau^3 v^3) \leq \lambda \leq 6A/(\tau^3 v^3)$. For values of λ outside of this range, subsets of locations in R have zero density. In particular, for $\lambda > -12A/(\tau^3 v^3)$, the activity distribution becomes more peaked around (0,0) until, eventually, all the activity A is located at (0,0). For $\lambda > 6A/(\tau^3 v^3)$, a region forms around (0,0) where there are no activities. This region becomes larger as λ increases until, eventually, all the activity A is distributed evenly on the perimeter of R. Since the present analysis is for illustrative purposes, distributions where $\lambda < -12A/(\tau^3 v^3)$ and $\lambda > 6A/(\tau^3 v^3)$ are not considered.

Given equation 5.91, an activity distribution is characterized by specifying λ in terms of τ, v, and A. Figure 5-15 provides cross-sectional views (along the x-axis in figure 5-14) of activity distributions characterized by different values of λ. Part c of figure 5-15 (where $\lambda = 0$) corresponds to the homogeneous–activity distribution analyzed in previous cases.

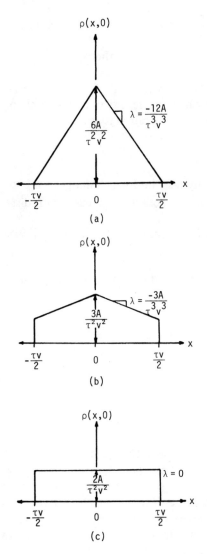

Figure 5-15. Examples of Different Activity Distributions.

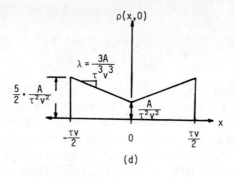

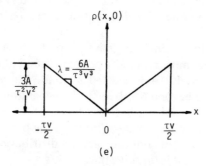

Figure 5–15 (*continued*).

Accessibility–benefit measures are now developed for activity distributions characterized by different values of λ. These measures have the form expressed in equation 5.30 with

$$u(T_{xy}) = cT_{xy} \tag{5.92}$$

and

$$q(d_{xy}) = \begin{cases} 1 & \text{for } (x, y) \\ 0 & \text{otherwise} \end{cases} \tag{5.93}$$

Recall that equation 5.92 implicitly assumes that the marginal value of the maximum amount of time available at a location is constant, and equation 5.93 implicitly assumes no distance discounting. The general form for the benefit measure considered here is

$$BM_6 = c \iint\limits_{(x,y) \in R} T_{xy}\, \varrho(x, y)\, dy dx \tag{5.94}$$

For $-12/(\tau^3 v^3) \le \lambda \le -6A/(\tau^3 v^3)$, equation 5.94 simplifies to

$$BM_6 = c\left[\frac{\varrho_0 \tau^3 v^3}{6} + \frac{\lambda \tau^4 v^3}{24}\right] \qquad (5.95)$$

Figure 5-16 plots BM_6 versus λ for $-12/(\tau^3 v^3) \le \lambda \le 6A/(\tau^3 v^3)$. The values of BM_6 for the five examples of activity distributions illustrated in figure 5-15 are represented in figure 5-16. Notice that as λ decreases, the density of activities at locations near the individual's origin and destination location (that is, near (0,0)) increase, and therefore, BM_6 increases. Also notice that the value of BM_6 for the activity distribution characterized by the peak in part a is one and one-half times as large as the value of BM_6 for the homogeneous activity distribution in part c and is twice as large as the value of BM_6 for the activity distribution characterized by the valley in part e.

As λ becomes increasingly negative beyond $-12A/(\tau^3 v^3)$, the activity distribution becomes more and more peaked around (0,0) until, in the limit, the total level of activity A is located at (0,0). Moreover, as λ becomes increasingly positive beyond $6A/(\tau^3 v^3)$, the geographical region surrounding (0,0), having no activities, becomes larger until, in the limit, the total level of activity A is uniformly distributed on the perimeter of the region R in figure 5-14. Given these limiting activity distributions and the assumptions underlying BM_6, it is intuitive that

$$\lim_{\lambda \to -\infty} BM_6 = \tau A \qquad (5.96)$$

and

$$\lim_{\lambda \to \infty} BM_6 = 0 \qquad (5.97)$$

Figure 5-16 illustrates how an individual's accessibility and, therefore, the value he imputes from a behavioral space depends on the spatial distribution of activities within this space. We now want to examine how the relative accessibility impacts of temporal and velocity strategies change with activity distributions. This is illustrated in figure 5-17, where the proportional change in v required to produce the same marginal benefit as a $\partial \tau$ change in τ is plotted as a function of λ. The five examples of activity distributions in figure 5-15 are represented in figure 5-17.

Notice that as attractive activities become located closer to the individual, the *relative* advantage of a temporal strategy over a velocity strategy increases. In addition, as attractive activities become located at more out-of-the-way locations, velocity strategies increase in importance. Moreover,

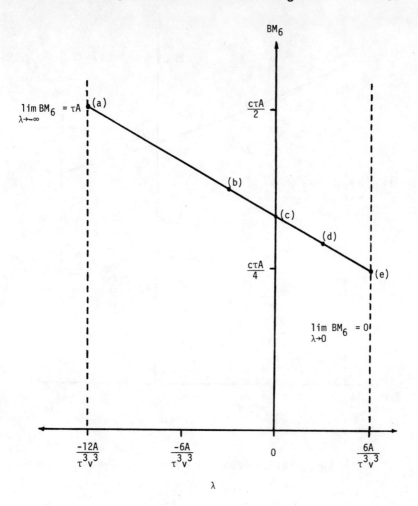

Figure 5–16. BM_6 versus λ Where Different Values of λ Represent Different Activity Distributions, as Illustrated in Figure 5–15.

notice that to induce a marginal benefit comparable to that induced by some change in τ, the individual's velocity would have to be changed

133 percent more when activities are distributed homogeneously as opposed to being peaked around the individual's location as in part a.

150 percent more when the activity distribution is characterized by the valley in part e as opposed to the peak in part a.

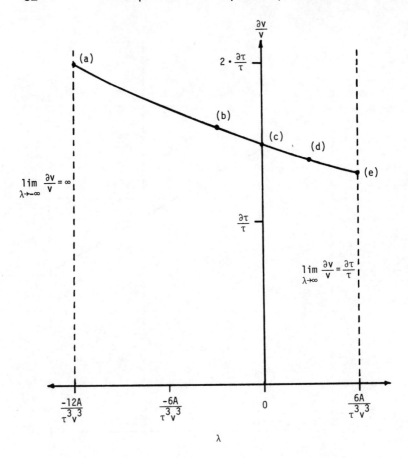

Figure 5-17. $\partial v/v$ versus λ for a Given $\partial \tau/\tau$.

For values of $\lambda < -12A/(\tau^3 v^3)$, the activity distribution becomes more peaked around (0,0), and even greater changes in v are required to induce a comparable marginal benefit as some change in v. In the limit, the total activity level A is located at (0,0) and changes in v will not increase the individual's accessibility. Therefore,

$$\lim_{\lambda \to -\infty} \frac{\partial v}{v} = \infty \qquad (5.98)$$

For values of $\lambda > 6A/(\tau^3 v^3)$, activities become more densely distributed at locations farther away from (0,0), and therefore, the change in velocity required to induce a comparable marginal benefit as some change in τ

becomes smaller. However, keep in mind that independent of how activities are distributed, v must always be changed by at least the same percent as τ to induce a comparable marginal benefit. Thus

$$\lim_{\lambda \to \infty} \frac{\partial v}{v} = \frac{\partial \tau}{\tau} \tag{5.99}$$

Figures 5-16 and 5-17 reflect the essence of the manner in which the accessibility implications of temporal and velocity strategies vary with respect to the spatial distribution of activities. The activity distributions corresponding to these figures in no way exhaust the possible idealized activity distributions that could be developed. Other possible activity distributions include those where the density of activities

Is constant along one dimension of a grid network and either increases or decreases linearly along the other dimension (figures 5-18a, b, and c).

Decreases linearly in both directions along one dimension of a grid network and increases linearly in one direction and decreases linearly in the other direction along the other dimension (figure 5-18d).

Decreases and/or increases nonlinearly in different directions along different dimensions.

Varies randomly over the geographical region encompassing an individual's behavioral space.

Varies systematically around a number of different centers within the geographical region encompassing an individual's behavioral space.

Each of these activity distributions lends itself to analysis using the approach developed herein.

It is beyond the scope of this case to analyze these different activity distributions in detail. They are listed here only to emphasize the fact that the paradigm underlying this research can be applied to assess the accessibility implications of different strategies for a broad variety of activity distributions.

In summary, in cases 1 through 5 it is assumed that activities are homogeneously distributed over the geographical region encompassing an individual's behavioral space. Here, this simplifying assumption is relaxed in order to examine the manner in which (1) the accessibility benefits an individual may realize from his behavioral space varies with the spatial distribution of activities within this space, and (2) the accessibility implications of temporal and velocity strategies vary with respect to different spatial distributions of activities.

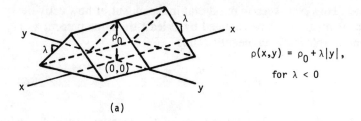

$$\rho(x,y) = \rho_0 + \lambda|y|,$$
$$\text{for } \lambda < 0$$

(a)

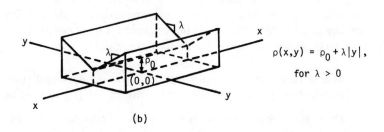

$$\rho(x,y) = \rho_0 + \lambda|y|,$$
$$\text{for } \lambda > 0$$

(b)

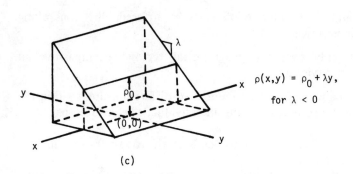

$$\rho(x,y) = \rho_0 + \lambda y,$$
$$\text{for } \lambda < 0$$

(c)

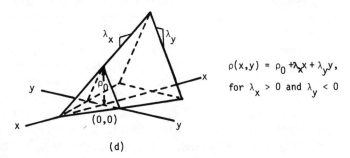

$$\rho(x,y) = \rho_0 + \lambda_x x + \lambda_y y,$$
$$\text{for } \lambda_x > 0 \text{ and } \lambda_y < 0$$

(d)

Figure 5-18. Other Examples of Activity Distributions.

Accessibility-benefit measures are developed based on different distributions of a fixed amount of total activity over the geographical region encompassing an individual's behavioral space. Based on these measures, it is concluded that

1. The accessibility benefits an individual realizes from his behavioral space increase as the density of activities at locations near the individual's origin increase.
2. If activities that are more attractive to an individual are at locations in close proximity, the *relative* advantage of a temporal strategy over a velocity strategy is greater than if activities are distributed homogeneously.
3. If activities that are more attractive to an individual are at out-of-the-way locations, the relative advantage of temporal strategies over velocity strategies is less than when activities are distributed homogeneously.

Finally, it is argued that the paradigm underlying this research can be applied to assess the accessibility implications of different strategies for a broad variety of activity distributions.

Case 7: Route-Opportunity Approach

The accessibility-benefit measures developed and analyzed in the previous cases all have the general form

$$f[(d_k, a_k, T_k)_{k \in R} = \sum_{k \in R} q(d_k) \cdot a_k \cdot u(T_k) \qquad (5.100)$$

These measures are based on location opportunities defined in terms of

1. The maximum amount of time an individual can spend at the location of an opportunity (T_k).
2. The level of activity at this location (a_k).
3. The distance that must be traveled to reach this location (d_k).

Opportunities can also be defined in terms of the routes (that is, paths through geographical space) encompassed by a space-time prism. This case develops accessibility-benefit measures based on such a conceptualization of an opportunity.

The general form of an accessibility-benefit measure defined over a set of *route* opportunities is specified in equation 4.15. Of particular interest here are measures in which the binary operation in equation 4.15 is the max operation. Measures based on the max operation assume that the value an individual derives from a set of route opportunities is equivalent to the value he derives from the route opportunity with the greatest value in the set.

Using the max operation in developing accessibility-benefit measures from a set of route opportunities is analogous to using economic utility theory to model the decisionmaking of individuals regarding routes and to infer the value an individual derives from a set of routes.[5] Utility theory postulated the following:

1. A value or utility can be assigned to each route encompassed by a space-time prism.
2. An individual confronted with a space-time prism will traverse the route that offers the greatest utility.
3. The utility derived from the most valuable route is the utility the individual derives from the entire set of routes available to him.

By equating the value of a set of route opportunities to the value derived from the route the individual would decide to traverse, utility theory allows inferences to be made regarding the values of individuals from observations of their behavior.

As in all previous cases, the analysis presented here is based on idealized conditions which capture the essence of the problems being addressed while simplifying them considerably. Specifically, consider an individual who (1) is free to leave location i at time t_i^1, (2) must retun to location i by time t_i^2, and (3) has a mode available at all times that operates at a constant maximum velocity v. The amount of time the individual has available to allocate to locations other than location i is

$$\tau = t_i^2 - t_i^1 \qquad (5.101)$$

For purposes of illustration, assume that activities exist *only* at locations along a single geographical path P which originates at i. Define path P in terms of the set of locations it connects. It is specifically being assumed here that

$$a_k = 0 \qquad \text{for all } k \notin P \qquad (5.102)$$

This assumption is analogous to a situation in which an individual lives at the end of a long narrow island.

The space-time prism corresponding to this case is depicted in figure 5-19. The horizontal axis in this figure represents path P. Even though P may be circuitous, it can be represented as a straight line without loss of generality. Since the individual would not consider traveling to locations

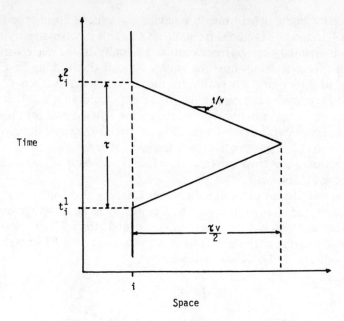

Figure 5-19. Space–Time Prism for Case 7.

where no activity exists, the prism in figure 5-19 delineates only time periods that the individual could spend at locations along path P.

Consider locations along path P to be continuous rather than discrete. Under this condition, routes can be uniquely defined along path P in terms of distances from i. Specifically, let x equal the distance from i along path P. The route corresponding to the distance x is defined in terms of the locations accessed when this distance is traversed. Denote this route as L_x, where L_x equals the set of locations along path P that are within the distance x from i.

Let $a(x)$ = a finite nonnegative real number representing a vector of attributes characterizing all the locations along route L_x

$s(x)$ = the amount of time the individual has available to allocate to
activities at locations along route L_x

The route opportunity corresponding to the route L_x is an ordered triad $[x, a(x), s(x)]$. The set of route opportunities available to the individual confronted with the space–time prism in figure 5-19 is

$$\overline{C}_P = \left\{[x, a(x), s(x)] \mid x/v \le \tau\right\} \qquad (5.103)$$

An accessibility–benefit measure having the general form specified in equation 4.15 can be developed from the set $\overline{C}_P$. This involves specifying the value an individual derives from each opportunity in the set $\overline{C}_P$ and an operation that determines how the values of each opportunity in $\overline{C}_P$ are combined to determine the overall value the individual derives from $\overline{C}_P$.

Initially, consider the case in which the opportunity $[x, a(x), s(x)]$ is equivalent to the opportunity represented by the ordered pair $[a(x), s(x)]$. This is comparable to assuming that distance affects the value of an opportunity only to the extent that it affects the level of activity accessed and the amount of time spent traveling (and therefore the amount of time available for stopping at locations).

The specifications of the function a must satisfy two conditions. First, as x increases, the number of locations accessed by route L_x increases. This implies that $a(x)$ should increase with x. Second, for a given distance x, $a(x)$ should increase as the total level of activity along path P increases.

The value of $s(x)$ is defined specifically as

$$s(x) = \tau - 2x/v \qquad (5.104)$$

Observe that as x increases, $a(x)$ increases and $s(x)$ decreases. That is, as the distance traveled increases, the number of activities accessed increases, and the amount of time available to pursue these activities decreases.

The value the individual derives from each opportunity in the set $\overline{C}_P$ is specified here in the context of a utility function. In particular, the utility derived from traveling a distance x from i can be expressed in terms of the ordered pair $[a(x), s(x)]$. Let

$$U(x) = U[a(x), s(x)] \qquad (5.105)$$

represent this utility, where U is a monotomically increasing function of $a(x)$ and $s(x)$. This function defines the value an individual derives from having the opportunity of allocating the amount of time $s(x)$ to the aggregate activity level represented by $a(x)$. The individual must decide how far to travel. Since $a(x)$ increases with x and $s(x)$ decreases with x, the individual must tradeoff accessing activities for time spent stopped at these activities.

Utility theory postulates that the individual will select x to maximize his utility. This optimal value of x is determined by solving

$$\max_x U[a(x), s(x)] \qquad (5.106)$$

subject to

$$x < \tau v/2 \qquad (5.107)$$

The preceding problem can be solved by specifying the function U and approximating the function a with a function continuous in x. A specification of U consistent with the power-function (or Cobb–Douglas function)[6] specification commonly used in economics is

$$U[a(x), s(x)] = \mu a(x)s(x)^{\alpha} \tag{5.108}$$

where μ and α are parameters such that $\mu > 0$ and $0 < \alpha < 1$. Observe that

1. U is nondecreasing in $a(x)$ and $s(x)$.
2. $U[0, s(x)] = 0$.
3. $U[a(x), 0] = 0$.
4. $\dfrac{dU[a(x), s(x)]}{ds(x)}$ diminishes as $s(X)$ increases

The value of $a(x)$ is not raised to a power in equation 5.108 because the meaning of $a(x)$ does not change with monotone transformations. An approximation of the function a that is continuous in x and satisfies the two conditions for this function noted earlier is

$$a(x) = (cx^{\Psi})^{\Phi} \tag{5.109}$$

where $c > 0$, $\Psi > 0$, and $0 < \Phi < 1$. The values of c and Ψ together define the spatial distribution of activities along P. The value of Φ defines the value the individual derives from accessing locations relative to the value he derives from spending time at these locations. Notice that

1. The larger the value of c, the greater the absolute level of activity along P.
2. If $0 < \Psi < 1$, the density of activities diminishes and asymptotically approaches zero with distance from location i.
3. If $\Psi = 1$, the density of activities is constant.
4. If $\Psi > 1$ the density of activities increases with distance from location i.

Also notice that $a(0) = 0$; that is, if the individual does not travel at all, he will not access any activities. One might argue that $a(0)$ should equal the level of activity at location i (that is, a_i). However, since locations are viewed here as continuous over P rather than discrete, activities exist over intervals along P rather than at specific points on P. Thus the level of activity at any specific point on P, such as $x = 0$, is zero.

Substituting equations 5.104 and 5.109 into equation 5.108 yields

$$U(x) = \mu(cx^{\Psi})^{\Phi}(\tau - 2x/v)^{\alpha} \tag{5.110}$$

Equation 5.110 is defined for all $x < \tau v/2$. Utility theory postulates that the distance the individual would decide to travel is determined by maximizing $U(x)$ in equation 5.110 with respect to x. The resulting optimal value of x, denoted x^*, is

$$x^* = \frac{1}{1 + \zeta} \cdot \frac{\tau v}{2} \qquad (5.111)$$

where $\zeta = \alpha/(\Psi\Phi)$. Notice that x^*

1. Varies linearly with the amount of time the individual has available (τ).
2. Varies linearly with the maximum speed the individual can travel (v).
3. Varies with the distribution of activities relative to location i (that is, varies with Ψ).
4. Does not depend on the absolute level of activity along P (that is, does not depend on c).
5. Varies with the ratio of the importance of the time and activity components of utility (that is, varies with α/Φ).

Figure 5-20 plots x^* versus Ψ for different values of α/Φ. This figure indicates, as one would expect, that (1) the individual will travel farther the farther activities are from location i (that is, the larger Ψ is), and (2) as the importance of the time component of utility increases relative to the importance of the activity component (that is, as α/Φ increases), the individual travels less.

Equation 5.111 can be rewritten to express the optimal amount of time the individual spends traveling (that is, $2x/v$). Specifically,

$$2x^*/v = \frac{1}{1 + \zeta} \cdot \tau \qquad (5.112)$$

Thus the amount of time the individual spends traveling increases linearly with the amount of time he has available and does not depend on the speed he can travel. This latter analytical result is consistent with empirical observations suggesting that individuals have fixed travel–time budgets (that is, that individuals allocate the same amount of time to travel independent of the speed they can travel).[7]

Substituting x^* in equation 5.111 into equation 5.108 gives

$$U(x^*) = \mu \left\{ c \left[\frac{\tau v}{2(1 + \zeta)} \right]^\Psi \right\}^\Phi \left(\frac{\zeta \tau}{1 + \zeta} \right)^\alpha \qquad (5.113)$$

Equation 5.113 is an indirect utility function. It represents the maximum utility the individual derives from the set of trajectories delineated by the

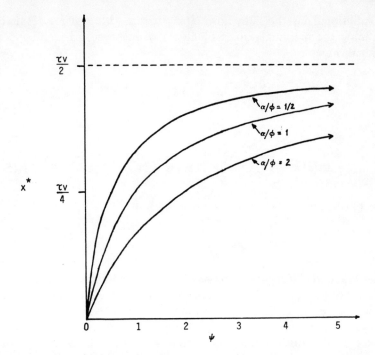

Figure 5-20. Optimal Travel Distance (x^*) versus Spatial Distribution of Activities (Ψ).

prism in figure 5-19. As such, it is an *accessibility-benefit measure.* The left term in parentheses on the right hand side of equation 5.113 is the total level of activity accessed by the individual when he travels the optimal distance x^* from i. The right term in parentheses on the righthand side of equation 5.113 is the total amount of time the individual spends stopped when he travels this optimal distance.

Of interest here is how $U(x^*)$ varies with τ and v. Notice that a change in τ changes both the amount of time the individual spends stopped and the total level of activity the individual accesses. In contrast, a change in v changes only the total level of activity the individual accesses. This results because the individual spends a constant amount of time traveling independent of v. Thus if v increases, he would travel farther without increasing the amount of time he spends traveling. This means he would access more activities without increasing the amount of time he spends traveling and, therefore, without decreasing the amount of time he spends stopped.

Additional insights into how $U(x^*)$ varies with τ and v result from examining the marginal values of $U(x^*)$ with respect to τ and v. These marginal values are

$$\frac{\partial U(x^*)}{\partial \tau} = K(\Psi\Phi + \alpha)v^{\Psi\Phi}\tau^{\Psi\Phi+\alpha-1} \qquad (5.114)$$

and

$$\frac{\partial U(x^*)}{\partial v} = K\Psi\Phi\tau^{\Psi\Phi+\alpha}v^{\Psi\Phi-1} \qquad (5.115)$$

respectively, where

$$K = \mu c^{\Phi}\left[\frac{1}{2(1+\varsigma)}\right]^{\Psi\Phi}\left(\frac{\varsigma}{1+\varsigma}\right)^{\alpha} \qquad (5.116)$$

Notice that $\partial U(x^*)/\partial \tau$ diminishes as τ increases only if $\Psi\Phi + \alpha < 1$. Under this condition, individuals with large values of τ would benefit less in an absolute sense from an increase in τ than individuals with small values of τ.

Furthermore, notice that $\partial U(x^*)/\partial v$ diminishes as v increases only if $\Psi\Phi < 1$. Under this condition, individuals with large values of v benefit less in an absolute sense from an increase in v than individuals with small values of v. The condition $\Psi\Phi < 1$ always holds whenever $\Psi \leq 1$, that is, whenever the density of activities is either constant or decreases with distance from location i.

The marginal rate of substitution (MRS) between τ and v can be determined from equations 5.153 ad 5.154. This MRS is the rate at which v must be substituted for τ to maintain a constant utility. Specifically,

$$\text{MRS} = \frac{\partial U(x^*)/\partial \tau}{\partial U(x^*)/\partial v} = (1+\varsigma)\frac{v}{\tau} \qquad (5.117)$$

Thus, as v increases, ever–smaller increases in τ are required to compensate for a change in v. Similarly as τ increases, ever–smaller increases in v are required to compensate for a change in τ.

The relative sensitivities of $U(x^*)$ with respect to changes in τ and v can be determined by comparing $\eta_\tau^{U(x^*)}$ and $\eta_v^{U(x^*)}$. Specifically,

$$\frac{\eta_\tau^{U(x^*)}}{\eta_v^{U(x^*)}} = 1+\varsigma \qquad (5.118)$$

Thus, as in all previous cases, a given percentage increase in τ will always result in a greater increase in accessibility than the same percentage increase in v. Furthermore, since $\varsigma = \alpha/(\Psi\Phi)$, a given temporal strategy becomes more attractive relative to a given velocity strategy as activities become located closer to i (that is, as Ψ decreases) and as the time component of utility becomes more important relative to the activity component of utility (that is, as α/Φ increases).

In summary, case 7 develops accessibility-benefit measures based on route opportunities. Such measures have the general form specified in equation 4.15. This general form involves specifying the value an individual derives from each route opportunity available to him and an operation that determines how the values of each available route opportunity are combined to determine the overall value the individual derives from all available routes.

Of particular interest here are accessibility-benefit measures specified in a manner analogous to using economic utility theory. This theory postulates the following:

1. That a value or utility can be assigned to each route encompassed by a space-time prism.
2. That an individual confronted with a space-time prism will traverse the route that offers the greatest utility.
3. That the utility derived from the most valuable route is the utility the individual derives from the entire set of routes available to him.

By equating the value of a set of route opportunities to the value derived from the route the individual would decide to traverse, utility theory allows inferences to be made regarding the values of individuals from observations of their behavior.

As in all previous cases, the analysis presented here is based on idealized conditions which capture the essence of the problems being addressed while simplifying them considerably. Specifically, this case considers an individual confronted with a space-time prism which delineates a set of routes of *different length* defined along the *same* geographical path. As such, routes are uniquely determined by distances from the individual's location or origin.

The approach taken here argues that the utility an individual derives from traveling a given distance from his origin can be defined in terms of the total level of activity accessed by traveling this distance and the total amount of time available to allocate to these activities. As the distance the individual travels increases, the level of activity accessed increases and the amount of time available to pursue these activities decreases (because the time spent traveling increases). Thus, in deciding how far to travel, the individual must tradeoff accessing activities for time spent stopped at these activities.

Using a power-function (that is, Cobb-Douglas function) specification for the utility an individual derives from having a given amount of time available to pursue a given level of activity, an expression for the distance the individual would travel (that is, the optimal distance) is developed. This expression indicates that the distance the individual would travel varies

1. Linearly with the amount of time the individual has available.
2. Linearly with the maximum average speed the individual can travel.
3. With the distribution of activities relative to his point of origin.

An expression for the amount of time the individual would spend traveling (that is, the optimal amount of time to allocate to traveling) is also developed. This expression indicates that the amount of time the individual spends traveling varies linearly with the total amount of time the individual has available and does not depend on the speed he can travel. This latter analytical result is consistent with empirical observations suggesting that individuals have fixed travel-time budgets (that is, that individuals allocate the same amount of time to travel independent of the speed they can travel).

An accessibility-benefit measure is defined here in terms of the maximum utility the individual derives from spending time at locations (that is, in terms of the utility he derives from traveling an optimal distance). This measure provides analytical results that are qualitatively the same as results obtained in previous cases. Specifically, the measure indicates the following:

1. That a given percentage increase in the amount of time an individual has available will always result in greater accessibility than the same percentage increase in the speed he can travel.
2. That the accessibility benefits an individual realizes from his behavioral space increase as the density of activities near his origin increases.
3. That the relative advantage of a temporal strategy over a velocity strategy increases as more attractive activities become located closer to an individual.

Since the measures developed in this case are based on assumptions about individual's valuations of opportunities that are quite different from the valuation assumptions underlying cases 2 through 6, the consistency of the qualitative results obtained from this case with those obtained in previous cases significantly increases the robustness of these results.

Case 8: Allocation of Time to Activities

Case 8 illustrates the utility approach to developing accessibility-benefit measures from a set of route opportunities defined by a space-time prism.

A route opportunity is defined relative to a finite, nonnegative number representing an aggregation of the attribute vectors of all locations accessed by a route. The value derived by an individual from a route opportunity is specified to depend on this number and the amount of time the individual has available to pursue activities.

This case employs utility theory (1) to model decisions of individuals regarding the amounts of time to spend pursuing activities at different locations along a given route, and (2) to illustrate the implications of these time-allocation decisions with respect to measuring accessibility benefits. This case demonstrates how individuals might ultimately select a trajectory to follow and how time and the characteristics of locations accessed by a route combine to determine the overall value an individual might derive from a route.

As in all previous cases, the analysis presented here is based on idealized conditions which capture the essence of the problems being addressed while simplifying them considerably. Specifically, consider an individual who

1. Is free to leave location i at time t_i.
2. Must arrive at location j by time t_j.
3. Has a mode available at all times that operates at a constant maximum velocity v.

Let d represent the distance from location i to location j, and let τ represent the amount of time the individual has available (that is, $\tau = t_j - t_i$). The space–time prism corresponding to these conditions encompasses an infinite number of trajectories that the individual could follow and still satisfy the constraints he confronts. Each possible trajectory is characterized by a sequence of stops at different locations and the durations of these different stops. Four exemplary trajectories are depicted in figure 5-21.

Given the trajectories encompassed by a space–time prism, the individual ultimately selects a single trajectory to follow. This decision–making process is modeled here using utility theory. To initially illustrate the applicability of the utility approach, consider the idealized case in which activities are available only at locations along the direct geographical path from location i to location j. Let L represent this set of locations. It is specifically being assumed here that

$$a_k = 0 \qquad \text{for all } k \notin L$$

where (as in previous cases) a_k is a nonnegative real number representing a vector of attributes characterizing location k. This assumption implies that the individual would not consider traveling to any location that is not in the set L. As such, the individual would never incur a travel time in excess of the

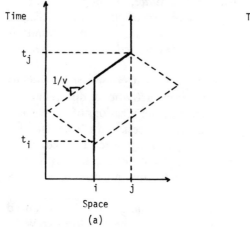
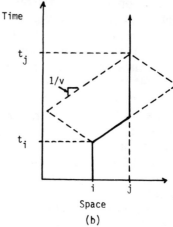

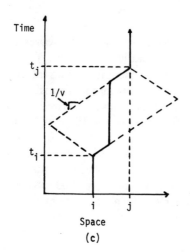
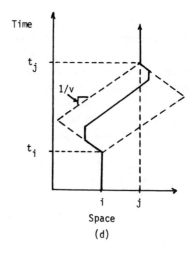

Figure 5-21. Examples of Trajectories.

time it takes to travel directly from location i to location j (that is, in excess of d/v).

The trajectories available to the individual under the preceding conditions are encompassed in the behavioral space depicted in figure 5–22. Since

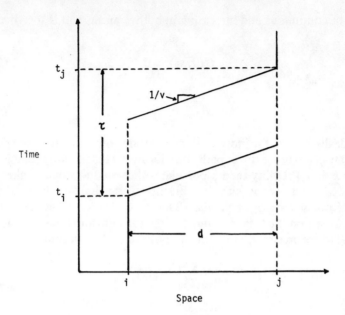

Figure 5–22. Space–Time Prism for Case 8.

the individual would not consider traveling to locations where no activity exists, the behavioral space in figure 5-22 only delineates trajectories defined over locations in the set L. Utility theory postulates that the trajectory the individual will follow is the one that maximizes a value function defined over the set of trajectories in his behavioral space. This value function is termed a *utility function*.

It is implicitly assumed here that activities are continually available in time and, therefore, that the individual would not backtrack when traveling from location i to location j. (In reality, the availability of activities varies with the time of day. However, assessing the travel and accessibility implications of temporal activity distributions exceeds the scope of this study and is therefore relegated to future research.) As such, the amounts of time the individual decides to spend at each reachable location uniquely characterizes a trajectory. The utility derived from a trajectory can therefore be defined as the sum of the utilities derived from each stop defining this trajectory. Furthermore, since activity participation requires both activities and time, it is reasonable to assume that the utility derived from stopping at a location depends on the activities at this location and the amount of time spent there. Based on this assumption, the utility of stopping at location k can be expressed in functional notation as $U(a_k, s_k)$, where s_k is the amount of time the individual decides to spend at location k. The function U is defined to be continuous and increasing in both a_k and s_k and is specified such that

$$U(0, s_k) = 0 \qquad (5.120)$$

and

$$U(a_k, 0) = 0 \qquad (5.121)$$

In this idealistic case, the individual must decide how much time to spend at each location along the direct path from location i to location j (that is, each location $k \in L$). Utility theory postulates that the individual makes these time–allocation decisions with the objective of maximizing the total utility he gains from all the stops he makes. This maximization takes place subject to a constraint on the total amount of time the individual has available for stopping. More precisely, utility theory postulates that the individual will

$$\max_{s_k} \sum_{k \in L} U(a_k, s_k) \qquad (5.122)$$

subject to

$$\sum_{k \in L} s_k \leq \tau - d/v \qquad (5.123)$$

To determine values of s_k that solve the preceding mathematical program, the function U must be specified. Two common specifications of utility functions are considered here.[8] The first is

$$U(a_k, s_k) = a_k \log (1 + c s_k) \qquad (5.124)$$

where c is a scale parameter with inverse time units. This function is characterized by diminishing marginal utility with respect to s_k and constant marginal utility with respect to a_k.

The second specification considered here is the power function (sometimes referred to as the Cobb–Douglas function). Specifically,

$$U(a_k, s_k) = \mu a_k s^\alpha \qquad (5.125)$$

where μ and α are parameters. When α is between 0 and 1, this specification is characterized by diminishing marginal utility with respect to s_k; when α equals 1, this marginal utility is constant; and when α exceeds 1, it increases. The value of a_k is not raised to a power in this specification, since a_k is simply an index and its meaning does not change with monotonic transformations.

Substituting equations 5.124 into equation 5.122 gives

$$\max_{s_k} \sum_{k \in L} a_k \log (1 + cs_k) \qquad (5.126)$$

subject to

$$\sum_{k \in L} s_k \leq \tau - d/v \qquad (5.127)$$

Using a Lagrangian multiplier λ for the constraint, optimal values of s_k, denoted s_k^*, can be determined from the equations characterizing the necessary and sufficient conditions for a maximum. These equations are

$$\frac{ca_k}{1 + cs_k^*} - \lambda = 0 \qquad (5.128)$$

and

$$\tau - d/v - \sum_{k \in L} s_k^* = 0 \qquad (5.129)$$

Solving equation 5.128 for s_k^* gives

$$s_k^* = \frac{a_k}{\lambda} - \frac{1}{c} \qquad (5.130)$$

Summing both sides of equation 5.130 over $k \in L$ gives

$$\sum_{k \in L} s_k^* = \frac{\sum_{k \in L} a_k}{\lambda} - \frac{n}{c} \qquad (5.131)$$

where n equals the number of locations in L with values of $a_k > 0$. From equation 5.129,

$$\sum_{k \in L} s_k^* = \tau - d/v \qquad (5.132)$$

Thus,

$$\lambda = \frac{\sum_{k \in L} a_k}{\tau - d/v + \dfrac{n}{c}} \qquad (5.133)$$

The expression for λ represents the implicit value to the individual of having more time available to pursue activities. In essence, λ represents the marginal utility of time under the specific conditions of the problem specified in equations 5.126 and 5.127.

Equation 5.133 states that the marginal value of time depends on the aggregate level of activity along route L (that is, $\sum_{k \in L} a_k$) and the amount of time already available for participating in activities (that is, $\tau - d/v$). The greater the level of activity along route L, the greater the marginl utility of time. Furthermore, the more time the individual has available, the lower the marginal utility of time. Thus the marginal utility of time increases as the density of activities along route L increases and diminishes as τ and v increases.

It is important to recognize the difference between conventional measures of the value of time used to assess benefits of transportation improvements and the expression for the marginal utility of time in equation 5.133. In particular, conventional measures of the value of time are used to place monetary value on travel–time savings resulting from transportation improvements. Equation 5.133 suggests that such time savings are valued relative to the uses an individual can make of the time savings and relative to the amount of time the individual already has available. Such factors are not considered when estimates of the monetary value of time are made. This raises serious questions about the relevance of conventional monetary value of time measures and assessments of transportation benefits based on these measures.

Substituting the expression for λ in equation 5.133 into equation 5.130 gives

$$s_k^* = \frac{a_k}{\sum_{k \in L} a_k}(\tau - d/v + \frac{n}{c}) - \frac{1}{c} \qquad (5.134)$$

Thus the amount of time spent at each location depends on the relative attractiveness of each location and the total amount of time available for stopping. Notice that if activities are distributed uniformly along L, that is, if $a_k = a$ for all $k \in L$, then

$$s_k^* = \frac{\tau - d/v}{n} \qquad (5.135)$$

Under this condition, an equal amount of time would be spent at each location. Furthermore, if $a_k = 0$ for all locations except some location $k' \in L$, then all available time would be spent at location k'.

Sustituting the expression for s_k^* in equation 5.134 into the objective function in equation 5.126 gives

$$U_k^* = \sum_{k \in L} a_k \log \left[\frac{c a_k}{\displaystyle\sum_{k \in L} a_k} (\tau - d/v + \frac{n}{c}) \right] \qquad (5.136)$$

where U^* represents the value of the objective function in equation 5.126 evaluated at s_k^* for all $k \in L$. Finally, assuming (without loss of generality) that

$$\sum_{k \in L} a_k = 1 \qquad (5.137)$$

yields

$$U_k^* = \log \left[c(\tau - d/v) + n \right] - (- \sum_{k \in L} a_k \log a_k) \qquad (5.138)$$

The function U^* is an indirect utility function. It is the value the individual derives from the best or optimal trajectory encompassed by the space–time prism in figure 5–22. In the context of utility theory, the value of this optimal trajectory represents the value the individual derives from the entire set of trajectories available to him. As such U^* is referred to here as an *accessibility–benefit measure*.

The expression for U^* in equation 5.138 has two distinct components. The component on the right is related to the distribution of activities along the route L. The component on the left is related to the amount of time the individual has available to allocate to stops. Since $\sum_{k \in L} a_k = 1$, the activity-distribution component can be interpreted using a concept from information theory known as *entropy*. The use of entropy in describing spatial interactions has been explored extensively by Wilson and his colleagues.[9] A general explanation of entropy in terms of utility-maximizing decision processes is given by Beckmann and Golob.[10]

The entropy expression in equation 5.138 is considered to be related to the possible role of uncertainty in the value an individual derives from the opportunities he has available in space–time. This entropy expression attains a maximum value in the case of relatively uniform values of a_k. Therefore, the accessibility–benefit measure is a minimum when activities at locations are nearly identical. However, when the distribution of activities is skewed toward a few locations with large attractions, entropy is less and the total accessibility–benefit measure is greater. Thus the more certain the individual is about where to spend his time, the greater the value he derives from the opportunities he has available.

The second component of U^* in equation 5.138 increases monotonically with the amount of time the individual has available for stops. This component is characterized by having diminishing marginal value with respect to increases in τ and v. Specifically,

$$\frac{\partial U^*}{\partial \tau} = \frac{c}{c(\tau - d/v) + n} \qquad (5.139)$$

and

$$\frac{\partial U^*}{\partial v} = \frac{cd}{v^2[c(\tau - d/v) + n]} \qquad (5.140)$$

Thus, in contrast to the measures developed and analyzed in cases 2 through 6, the measure developed in this case suggests that individuals in more flexible situations (that is, individuals confronted with large values of τ and v) benefit less in an *absolute* sense from increases in τ and v than individuals who are more constrained.

Notice that under the assumption in equation 5.137, the marginal value of U^* with respect to τ (equation 5.139) equals λ. In fact, independent of an assumption about the value of the total level of activity along route L, the marginal value of U^* with respect to τ equals λ. This follows directly from the definition of λ.

Equations 5.139 and 5.140 can be used to determine the marginal rate of substitution (MRS) for utility between τ and v. This MRS is the rate at which v must be substituted for τ to maintain a constant utility. Specifically,

$$\text{MRS} = \frac{\dfrac{\partial U^*}{\partial \tau}}{\dfrac{\partial U^*}{\partial d}} = \frac{v^2}{d} \qquad (5.141)$$

Thus, as v increases, smaller and smaller increases in τ are required to compensate for a change in v. This result holds independent of the spatial distribution of acitivities along route L. Also notice that MRS is independent of τ and decreases as the distance the individual has to travel increases (that is, as d increases).

The marginal rate of substitution allows assessment of the *absolute* sensitivity of U^* with respect to τ and v. As in cases 2 through 7, interest also lies in assessing the *relative* sensitivity of U^* with respect to τ and v. This is accomplished by comparing $\eta_\tau^{U^*}$ and $\eta_v^{U^*}$. Specifically,

$$\frac{\eta_\tau^{U^*}}{\eta_v^{U^*}} = \frac{\tau}{d/v} = \beta \qquad (5.142)$$

where, as described in case 2, β is a measure of the degree to which an individual is constrained in space–time. Specifically, the larger the value of β, the more flexible the individual is.

Equation 5.142 is qualitatively consistent with results obtained in cases 2 through 7. It indicates (1) that a given percentage increase in τ will always result in a greater increase in accessibility than the same percentage increase in v, and (2) that the less constrained an individual's freedom in space and time, the greater the attractiveness of a strategy that increases τ to a strategy that increases v.

Similar results are obtained using the power–function specification of U in equation 5.125. Specifically, substituting equation 5.125 into equation 5.122 gives

$$\max_{s_k} U(a_k, s_k) = \max_{s_k} \sum_{k \in L} \mu a_k s_k{}^{\alpha} \qquad (5.143)$$

subject to

$$\sum_{k \in L} s_k \leq \tau - d/v \qquad (5.144)$$

The solution to the preceding problem is trivial when $\alpha \geq 1$. In this case, the individual would spend all his available time at the location having the greatest value of a_k. As such, only the case where $0 < \alpha < 1$ is of interest here. In this case, the marginal value of stopping at a location diminishes as the amount of time spent there increases. This same property is provided by the logarithmic utility function analyzed previously.

Again, using the Lagrangian multiplier λ for the constraint, expressions for the optimal values of s_k and λ can be determined when $0 < \alpha < 1$. These expressions are

$$\lambda = \frac{\mu \alpha \sum_{k \in L} (a_k{}^{1/(1-\alpha)})^{1-\alpha}}{(\tau - d/v)^{1-\alpha}} \qquad (5.145)$$

and

$$s_k^* = \frac{a_k{}^{1/(1-\alpha)}}{\sum_{k \in L} a_k{}^{1/(1-\alpha)}}(\tau - d/v) \qquad (5.146)$$

Equations 5.145 and 5.146 are similar in form and have the same implications as equations 5.133 and 5.134, respectively. The indirect utility function resulting from substituting equation 5.146 into the objective function in equation 5.143 is

$$U^* = \mu \left[\sum_{k \in L} (a_k{}^{1/(1-\alpha)})^{1-\alpha} \right] (\tau - d/v)^{\alpha} \qquad (5.147)$$

As in the expression for U^* in equation 5.136, the marginal values of the preceding expression for U^* with respect to τ and v decrease as τ and v increase. Specifically,

$$\frac{\partial U^*}{\partial \tau} = \lambda \qquad (5.148)$$

and

$$\frac{\partial U^*}{\partial v} = \frac{\lambda d}{v^2} \qquad (5.149)$$

Thus, as with equation 5.139 and 5.140, results in equation 5.148 and 5.149 suggest that individuals in more flexible situations (that is, individuals confronted with large values of τ and v) benefit less in an absolute sense from increases in τ and v than individuals who are more constrained.

The MRS for utility between τ and v and the ratio of the elasticities of U^* with respect to τ and v when the power–function specification is used are

$$\text{MRS} = \frac{v^2}{d} \qquad (5.150)$$

and

$$\frac{\eta_\tau^{U^*}}{\eta_v^{U^*}} = \frac{\tau}{d/v} = \beta \qquad (5.151)$$

These expressions are identical with the expressions for MRS and the ratio of elasticities obtained when the logarithmic specification in equation 5.124 is used. As such, they have identical interpretations.

In summary, case 8 employs utility theory (1) to model decisions of individuals regarding the amounts of time to spend pursuing activities at different locations along a given route, and (2) to illustrate the implications of these time–allocation decisions with respect to measuring accessibility benefits. In so doing, this case demonstrates how individuals might ultimately select a trajectory to follow and how time and the characteristics of locations accessed by a route combine to determine the overall value an individual might derive from a route.

To illustrate the utility approach to modeling time–allocation decisions of individuals, this case considers an individual in an idealized setting in which all activities are located along the direct route from his origin to his destination. A result of this idealized setting is that the individual does not have to go out of his way to reach locations of activities and therefore does not have to consider time and money costs of travel when allocating his time to activities at different locations.

The amounts of time the individual decides to spend at each reachable location is viewed here as uniquely characterizing a trajectory. As such, the utility derived from a trajectory is considered to be the sum of the utilities derived from each stop defining this trajectory. Furthermore, since activity participation requires both activities and time, it is assumed here that the utility derived from stopping at a location depends on the activities at this location and the amount of time spent there.

Two common specifications of the utility of stopping at locations are used in this case (one that is logarithmic in time and multiplicative in activities and one that is known as the power function). Both specifications result in indirect utility functions that represent the utility the individual derives from the best or optimal trajectory available to him and, therefore, the value he derives from the entire set of trajectories available to him.

In contrast to the accessibility–benefit measures developed and analyzed in cases 2 through 6, the indirect utility functions developed in this case suggest that individuals in more flexible situations (that is, individuals who can travel fast or have large blocks of discretionary time available) benefit less in an *absolute* sense from increases in their speed and available time than individuals who are more constrained. However, regarding the relative sensitivities of an individual's accessibility with respect to changes in his speed and available time, analytical results in this case are qualitatively the same as analytical results in cases 2 through 6. Specifically, results in this case indicate (1) that a given percentage increase in the amount of time an individual has available will always result in a greater increase in accessibility than the same percentage increase in the speed he can travel, and (2) that the less constrained an individual's freedom in space and time is, the greater the attractiveness of a strategy that increases the time he has available to a strategy that increases the speed he can travel.

Discussion of Results from Cases 1 through 8

The salient policy result emerging from this chapter is that temporal strategies (for example, flextime) have the potential of providing substantially greater increases in the accessibility of individuals than strategies directed toward increasing velocities (for example, strategies aimed at reducing congestion, such as facility expansions, pricing, or priorities for high–occupancy vehicles). This is especially true in light of the significant accomplishments already realized in the delivery of high–speed transportation services to most of the population.

It is important to recognize that this salient policy result is not based on benefit/cost or effectiveness/cost arguments. Rather it is based only on comparisons of the marginal accessibility benefits that individuals *may* accrue from strategies that either change the time constraints they confront or the velocities they can travel. While the costs of enacting such changes are not considered explicitly, temporal strategies such as flextime have little if any costs associated with them. In fact, many firms have recognized productivity gains and reduced absenteeism as a result of instituting flextime.[11] Transportation strategies, on the other hand, often entail substantial capital investments. Therefore, as with benefits, costs seem to favor selected temporal strategies. Clearly, this conjecture must be subjected to more rigorous analysis.

It is also important to recognize that the salient policy result of this study does not emerge from aggregating the marginal accessibility benefits resulting from temporal and velocity strategies over the whole population. Rather it is based on an evaluation of these strategies over the entire range of constraints that individuals could confront and the emergence of robust conclusions over this range.

While robust conclusions are obtained over the entire range of constraints, the extent to which temporal strategies dominate velocity strategies varies over this range. Specifically, the less constrained an individual is, the greater the attractiveness of a temporal strategy relative to a velocity strategy. For this reason, knowledge of the distribution of these constraints over the population would be helpful in assessing the distributional impacts of strategies. However, using this knowledge for purposes of attaining aggregate measures of changes in accessibility-benefits is inappropriate because of our inability to make interpersonal value comparisons. Furthermore, these aggregate measures would obscure important distributional insights.

If temporal strategies are so attractive relative to velocity strategies, why have velocity strategies been the primary focus of planners and policy-makers and (until recently) temporal strategies have recieved such little attention? To answer this question, consideration must be given to the public-sector nature of velocity strategies and the private-sector nature of temporal strategies. Velocity strategies typically require public decisions regarding investments in public goods such as highways and transit systems or the use of existing public facilities (for example, pricing and priority lanes). As a result, numerous special interest groups such as the Bureau of Public Roads, the construction industry, and the automobile industry have provided strong voices in favor of increasing velocities.[12] In contrast, the private market is quite conducive to generating temporal innovations. Being aware of the importance individuals place on saving time and being freed from time constraints, inventors and entrepreneurs have developed and successfully marketed numerous temporal innovations. Table 5-1 contains a list of such innovations and descriptions of their time-saving and/or time-freeing functions. Because such innovations do not require public action (beyond consumer protection) for their implementation, they have not demanded the attention of policymakers and planners.

Aside from the free market system, a voice for temporal strategies has existed for some time. In particular, labor unions have traditionally voiced the importance individuals place on discretionary time. One of the initial achievements of unions was the standard 40-hour, 5-day work week with compensation for overtime exceeding base wages. As depicted in figure 5-23, the standard work week has remained quite stable since World War II.[13] During this period, the priorities of unions were on wages, pensions, seniority rights, layoff protection, health care, and vacation time.

Attainment of these goals and the growing number of unions representing employees in the service sector have refueled the interests of unions and other interest groups (for example, the Department of Labor) in temporal strategies. In fact, large-scale annual conferences are being held on alternative work schedules.[14] Major participants in these conferences include representatives from unions, the Department of Labor, and women's groups.

Table 5-1
Examples of Innovations that Either Save Time or Free Individuals from Coupling Contraints

Innovation	Time-Saving or Time-Freeing Function
Refrigerator	Reduces the frequency of grocery shopping trips and the amount of time required for shopping.
Microwave ovens	Reduces the time required to prepare meals
Instant dinners	Reduces the time required to prepare meals
Timers on ovens	Allows for a meal to begin cooking without being present to turn on an oven
Automatic dishwashers	Reduces time spent washing dishes
Washing machines and tumble dryers	Reduces time spent cleaning clothes
Permanent press clothing	Eliminates need for ironing and therefore saves time
Videotape recorders for TV sets	Free individuals from contraints imposed by the scheduling of programs
Telephone	Reduces time required for communication (as well as travel)
Automatic telephone message recorder	Eliminates need for being at a telephone in order to receive a message
Day care centers	Free parents from selected childcare responsibilities

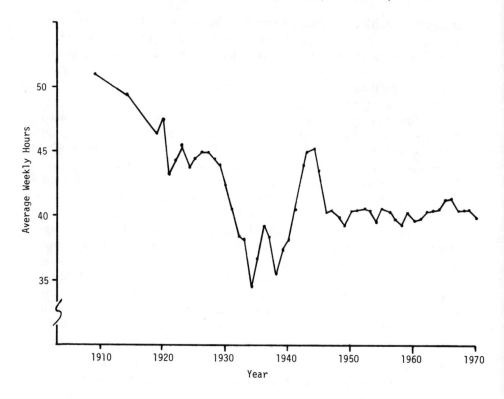

Figure 5-23. Historical Trend in Average Weekly Hours for Production
              Workers in Manufacturing.

Thus, while the temporal dimension of accessibility has not been the
focus of accessibility policymaking and is typically not viewed in accessibility terms, it has not been overlooked. Furthermore, as will be discussed in
chapter 6, current trends indicate that increasingly more attention is being
paid to temporal strategies. This increases the need for methodologies such
as the one developed in this study that systematically evaluate temporal
strategies in conjunction with transportation and spatial strategies.

Another policy result of particular interest here emerges from the fact
that the attractiveness of velocity strategies relative to temporal strategies
diminishes as the initial velocity of an individual increases. This means that
the larger one's initial velocity, the more this velocity must increase to
generate the same change in accessibility as some given increase in time
availability. Therefore, by *not* considering temporal strategies as alternatives to velocity strategies, transportation planners run the risk of overexploiting velocity strategies. Furthermore, the potential accessibility gains

resulting from velocity strategies relative to those resulting from temporal strategies are greatest for the segment of the population that is constrained to low-speed transportation services. This is precisely the segment of the population that policies emerging from conventional travel-volume-travel-time methodologies have neglected. The need for improving the transportation services of this segment is therefore paramount.

Additional policy results that are more specific in nature are summarized and discussed at the ends of the eight cases contained in this chapter. One of these results warranting further discussion here concerns the comparability of temporal strategies and velocity strategies as a means of enhancing accessibility in an energy-scarce world. In particular, it is demonstrated that as fuel prices increase, a given temporal strategy becomes increasingly more attractive relative to a given velocity strategy. The reason for this is that by increasing the per-mile monetary cost of travel, increased fuel prices reduce the value of opportunities at locations which are farther away. It is these distant locations that velocity strategies have the most favorable impacts on. As such, increasingly greater improvements in velocities are required to compensate for the reductions in accessibility that result from greater fuel prices. This is not the case with temporal strategies, because the relative advantage of temporal strategies over velocity strategies is greatest for opportunities located at proximate locations. Thus it becomes easier to compensate for accessibility reductions resulting from fuel price increases by allowing individuals to spend more time at nearby locations than by allowing them to reach distant locations faster.

The major contributions of this book are included in the methodological study of accessibility provided to this point. To supplement this methodological study, the following chapter provides some empirical insights concerning accessibility and the travel behavior of individuals in the context of the constraints they confront.

6 Empirical Considerations

This chapter serves three purposes. First, it provides typical values for the variables incorporated in the accessibility measures developed in chapters 4 and 5 and insights into historical trends in these values. Second, it assesses some observations that are commonly made regarding accessibility in the context of the data presented here and in the context of the present accessibility methodology. Finally, this chapter discusses the data needed for a detailed analysis of accessibility, how these data could be collected, and the questions to which they could be applied.

Typical Values and Historical Trends in Velocities, Distances, and Time Constraints

The fundamental variables incorporated in the accessibility measures developed here include

1. The maximum velocity individuals can sustain in overcoming geographical space (v).
2. The distances individuals typically travel between coupling constraints (for example, the distance from home to work)(d).
3. The time constraints of individuals (τ).

Typical values of these variables and insights into their historical trends are provided in the following discussions.

Velocities (v)

Underlying the accessibility measures developed here are the suppositions that an individual has unfettered access to private transportation (such as walking, a bicycle, or an automobile) and that this transportation allows travel at a constant maximum velocity over an idealized network at all times of the day. This is a very simple view of an individual's ability to overcome space. In reality, many individuals do not have unfettered access to private transportation (especially automobiles). Furthermore, if such access does exist, the maximum velocity an individual can sustain using these modes

111

varies with the time of day and precise location of the individual in relation to the network.

Although the view of transportation taken here is quite simple conceptually, it reflects the essence of how behavioral spaces are affected by transportation and therefore how different transportation strategies influence the accessibilities of individuals. Thus, from an empirical standpoint, emphasis is placed on the velocities individuals can expect to sustain when traveling in an automobile. Given that over 90 percent of the passenger miles traveled each year in the United States are by passenger car or truck, the insights gained from a brief examination of the speeds of automobiles have broad applicability. This focus on automobile speeds is not intended to suggest that the transportation problems of individuals without access to automobiles are of less importance. This is not the case. However, consideration of these special problems is beyond the scope of this limited empirical discussion.

While improving automobile speeds (that is, reducing congestion) has been a high-priority objective of urban transportation policy since World War II, surprisingly little data are available on how automobile speeds have changed over time. The most comprehensive survey of automobile speed trends in U.S. cities is provided by Koltnow.[1] Concerning national studies, Koltnow reports that (1) in 1949, the average peak and off-peak speeds in all cities with populations over 5,000 were 18.1 and 23.5 mi/h. respectively; and (2) in 1958, the average speed of commuters leaving the downtown areas of the twenty-five largest U.S. cities was 20 mi/h for the first 30 minutes of their trip.

To supplement Koltnow's information, results from the Nationwide Personal Transportation Study[2] are used to obtain a value for the nationwide average automobile speed of commuters in 1969-1970. Results from this survey include the average home-to-work commuting time of respondents using private transportation (automobile, taxi, or motorcycle) for different work trip lengths and the percent of all workers traveling each distance. These average travel times and distances provide approximations of average automobile speeds for different commute distances. These approximations are presented in table 6-1 and plotted against commute distance in figure 6-1. A nationwide average automobile speed for commuters is obtained by weighting the average speed for each commute distance by the percentage of commuters traveling each distance. The resulting average speed is 23.2 mi/h. (A speed of 40 mi/h was used for the average speed of commuters traveling more than 25 miles.)

Clearly, any direct comparisons of the 1949, 1958, and 1969-1970 nationwide average automobile speeds reported here are subject to numerous caveats regarding the comparability of the samples and methods

Table 6-1
Average Commute Times and Speeds for Different Home-to-Work Trip Lengths

Home-to-Work Trip Length (miles)	Average Commute Time for All SMSA Sizes (minutes)	Average Commute Speed (mi/h)	Percent of all Workers
½	6	5.00	2.1
1	8	7.50	8.1
2	11	10.90	9.5
3	12	15.00	9.1
4	15	16.00	6.9
5	16	18.75	10.5
6	18	20.00	4.8
7	20	21.00	5.4
8	22	21.80	5.1
9	23	23.50	2.5
10	24	25.00	8.2
11	27	24.40	1.5
12	28	25.70	4.3
13	25 [a]	31.20	1.5
14	30	28.00	1.5
15-19	32	31.90 [b]	8.7
20-24	36	36.70 [b]	5.0
25 and over	50	—	5.3

Source: U.S. Department of Transportation (1970).

[a] While this travel time deviates from the prior sequence of increasing travel times, it is nevertheless the value reported in the Nationwide Personal Transportation Study. A reason for this deviation is not available.

[b] Midpoint of the trip-length range is used to approximate commute speed.

used in obtaining them. Nevertheless, these direct comparisons are made to provide some interesting, albeit crude, insights into the historical trends of average nationwide automobile speeds within metropolitan areas.

The 1949 and 1969-1970 average speeds are both derived from nationwide samples drawn throughout metropolitan areas of all sizes, while the 1958 average speed is derived from trips originating in the downtown areas of the twenty-five largest U.S. cities. Like the 1949 results, average speeds in 1969-1970 had little variation over city size. Assuming that this was also the case in 1958, the fact that only large cities are represented in the 1958 sample should not bias the comparability of the 1958 speed to the other two speeds. However, since the 1958 sample consists of trips originating in downtown areas, the 1958 speed most likely reflects the worst example of urban commuting at that time. This is not the case with the 1949 and 1969-1970 peak-period speeds.

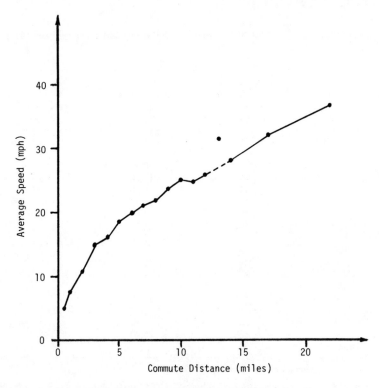

Figure 6-1. Average Speed versus Commute Distance for Commuters Using Private Transportation (Automobiles, Taxis, Motorcycles).

Even though the 1958 speed of 20 mi/h may be biased downward, it is 9.5 percent better than the average peak period speed of 18.1 mi/h noted in 1949. Furthermore, the 1969-1970 average commute speed of 23.2 mi/h is 28 percent greater than the 1949 average peak-period speed.

Thus, during a period in which the urban population of the United States increased approximately 54 percent, total vehicle miles traveled in U.S. urban areas increased approximately 163 percent, and U.S. automobile registration increased 121 percent, substantial improvements in the nationwide average peak-period automobile speed were still realized. Credit for these improvements is given to the development of urban freeway and expressway systems, improved traffic signal technology, the imposition and enforcement of parking regulations, arterial street improvements, and the large-scale use of traffic engineering measures such as one way streets, turning lanes, and turning prohibitions.

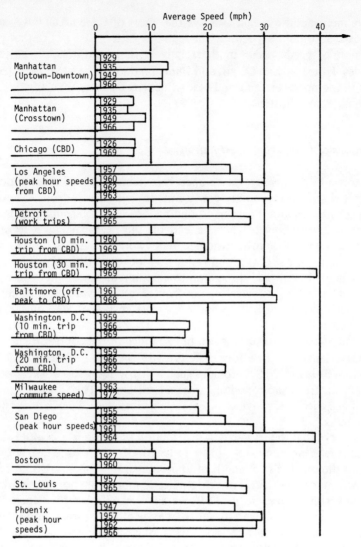

Source: Koltnow (1970).

Figure 6-2. Average Automobile Speeds in Selected U.S. Cities.

Since peak and off-peak average automobile speeds vary significantly across metropolitan areas, the nationwide averages presented here have little meaning when considering the scale and trends of automobile speeds in specific metropolitan areas. Koltnow[3] provides insights into the variability of average automobile speeds across metropolitan areas and historical trends of these speeds. Figure 6-2 summarizes Koltnow's findings for twelve metropolitan areas. Observe that most of these areas have enjoyed increased automobile speeds up through the sixties. Also notice that greater automobile speeds occur in the relatively new southwestern cities (Los Angeles, Houston, San Diego, and Phoenix) than in the older industrialized cities in the northeast and midwest (Chicago, Detroit, Washington, D.C., Milwaukee, and Boston).

Locations of Origins and Destinations

The accessibility measures developed here depend in part on the locations associated with the coupling constraints individuals confront. These coupling constraints and their corresponding locations determine the distances individuals *must* travel. They depend on the personal characteristics of individuals (for example, whether they work, attend school, and are parents; and their sex, age, and residential location). It is beyond the scope of this limited empirical discussion to examine distances between a broad variety of coupling constraints confronted by individuals with different characteristics. Instead, only home–to–work distances are considered for employed individuals.

Home–to–work distances can be examined in the context of home–to–work trip–length distributions. The 1969–1970 Nationwide Personal Transportation Study (NPTS)[4] provides such a distribution for workers sampled nationwide from metropolitan areas of all sizes. This distribution, presented in figure 6–3, provides initial insights into the scale of home–to–work trip lengths.

Observe that the trip–length distribution in figure 6–3 is quite skewed. In fact, the mean home–to–work trip length of 9.2 miles is nearly twice as large as the median trip length of approximately 5 miles. Also notice that 19.1 percent of all workers travel 15 miles or more from home to work.

Numerous factors influence home–to–work trip lengths.[5] Included are transportation systems, the structure and size of urban areas, and social and economic characteristics of individuals, such as income, sex, and ethnic background. As such, nationwide trip–length distributions have little meaning when considering the scale of home–to–work trip lengths of different individuals residing and working in different metropolitan areas.

The variability of home–to–work trip lengths across metropolitan areas is reflected in table 6–2, where the mean home–to–work trip length is presented for a variety of standard metropolitan statistical areas (SMSAs). The variability of home–to–work trip lengths with respect to the characteristics of individuals is illustrated in table 6–3, where the effect of an individual's sex on home–to–work trip lengths is summarized on a nationwide scale.

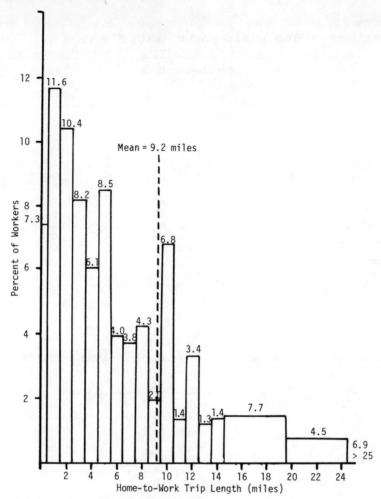

Source: U.S. Department of Transportation (1970).

Figure 6–3. Distribution of Home–to–Work Trip Lengths from the
Nationwide Personal Transportation Survey Sample.

While it is generally recognized that home–to–work distances have been
increasing over time, there is surprisingly little empirical evidence in the
form of trip–length distributions to document this conclusion. Nationwide
home–to–work trip–length distributions which are compatible with the
1969-1970 NTPS sample are unavailable. In addition, only a very limited
number of metropolitan areas have collected information which allows
assessment of trends in trip lengths. Two of these areas, Detroit and Milwaukee, are discussed here.

Table 6-2
Mean Home-to-Work Trip Lengths for Selected SMSAs

SMSA	Mean Home-to-Work Trip Length (miles)	Year of Study
Los Angeles (includes Orange and Ventura Counties)	8.89	—
Chicago	6.62	—
Philadelphia	4.40	1960
Detroit	6.60	1953
	7.75	1965
Washington	7.20	1968
Dallas	6.20	1964
Seattle	8.55	1970–71
Milwaukee	5.00	1963
	5.40	1972
Buffalo	3.70	1962
Kansas City	8.07	1970

Source: Barton–Aschman Associates, et al. (1974).

Table 6-3
Characteristics of Home-to-Work Trip-Length Distributions for Males and Females

	Male	Female
Mean	12.2 (mi)	6.8 (mi)
Median	5.4 (mi)	3.8 (mi)
Percent ≤ 5 mi	48	60

Source: Hummon (1976).

Bellomo, Dial, and Voorhees[6] provide a detailed historical analysis of trip lengths in the Detroit metropolitan area using data collected in 1953 and 1965. Figure 6-4 presents the auto-driver home-to-work trip-length distribution for both years. Observe that from 1953 to 1965, home-to-work trip lengths have generally increased; the mean length in 1965 being 18 percent greater than the mean length in 1953. During this same period, the number of work trips increased 26 percent and the average automobile commute speed increased 12 percent (see figure 6-2).

More recent but less complete data are available for Milwaukee. In particular, transportation studies performed by the Southeastern Wisconsin Regional Planning Commission in 1963 and 1972[7] indicate that the average home-to-work trip length in Milwaukee increased from 5.0 miles in 1963 to

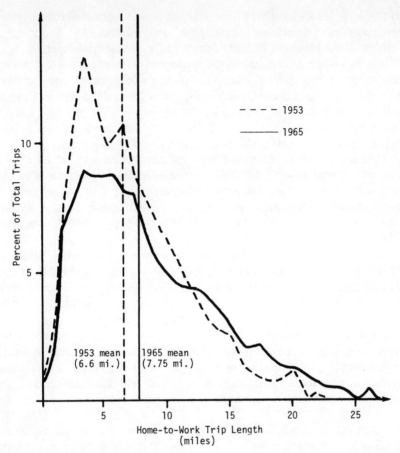

Source: Bellomo, Dial, and Voorhees (1970).

Figure 6-4. 1953 and 1965 Home-to-Work Trip-Length Distributions for Detroit.

5.4 miles in 1972 (an 8 percent increase). During this same period, average network speed increased 8 percent (from 16.8 mi/h in 1963 to 18.1 mi/h in 1972).

Time Constraints

The study of accessibility presented here is based on the premise that at any point in time, an individual's existence can be viewed in the context of an origin coupling constraint, a destination coupling constraint, and the transportation he has available. Coupling constraints are associated with activities that individuals have very little scheduling and locational control over. These constraints determine the blocks of time available for discretionary activities. These blocks of time are denoted here as *time constraints*.

It is important to distinguish the concept of a time constraint from the more common concepts of time use and time allocation.[8] *Time use* deals with actual behavior; that is, it is concerned with how individuals actually use their time. It does not encompass the alternative uses of time available to an individual. As such, studies of time use do not provide direct insights into the constraints individuals confront in using their time.

Time allocation is concerned with the mechanisms by which time is allocated, as well as with the consequences and opportunity costs of different alternatives. Time-allocation studies are usually approached through a demand and supply structure. There are several time-allocation schools in the field of economics, the best known evolving from the work of Becker.[9]

The concept of a time constraint is somewhat artificial. While all activities have the properties of duration, a position in time (that is, a start time), a place in a sequence of events, and a location or path in space, there are only a very limited set of activities that are coupling constraints in the truest sense (that is, obligatory activities that are rigidly fixed in space and time). For many individuals, work, school, and certain appointments (such as attending scheduled events) that an individual cannot schedule at discretion are coupling constraints. For most other activities, there is a variation in freedom of choice with regard to whether, where, when, and/or the duration of participation in activities. This makes assessment of time constraints a difficult task.

To an extent, the difficulties involved in assessing time constraints are not a major problem here. What is important at this point is recognizing the existence of time constraints and how they affect accessibility rather than determining the exact values of these constraints for individuals with different characteristics. This stems in part from the ability of the methodology developed and evaluated here to assess the accessibility implications of transportation, temporal, and spatial strategies over a wide range of time constraints and the robustness of the conclusions developed in the eight cases in chapter 5 over this range.

While direct observations of time constraints are currently unavailable, insights into the magnitude and variability of these constraints across individuals with different characteristics can be obtained from time-use studies. The most comprehensive data on how Americans use their time is found in a 1966 study conducted by Converse and Robinson.[10] The information presented in this study is organized by time budgets. A *time budget* describes the distribution of time spent by respondents performing various activities. The study defines thirty-seven basic activities and presents the distribution in terms of the average number of hours spent on each activity.

Hummon[11] has taken these daily time–budget data and presented them in a more aggregate form. In particular, Hummon collapses the thirty-seven activities into ten more general activities, and instead of reporting hours per day, he reports hours per week.

Table 6-4 presents the average weekly time budgets for employed married men, employed married women, and unemployed married women. The activities defining the rows in table 6-4 are defined as follows:

1. Work—a regular job, a second job, and nonwork–related activities, for example, coffee breaks.
2. Housework—preparing food, house cleaning, laundry, maintenance and upkeep of the house, gardening, and so on.
3. Personal care—sleeping, personal care, eating, and resting.
4. Child care.
5. Shopping.
6. Educational, religious, civic.
7. Mass media—listening to the radio, watching television, reading.
8. Social leisure—all social life activities such as conversation, walking, sports, theater, and so on.
9. Work travel.
10. Other travel.

As argued by Hummon, the first four activities in table 6-4 (that is, work, housework, personal care, and child care) are different from the

Table 6-4
Average Weekly Time Budgets of Married Men and Women in 1965

	Employed Men	Employed Women	Unemployed Women
Work	48.3	35.7	.7
Housework	4.2	22.4	35.7
Personal care	70.0	71.4	74.2
Child care	0.7	2.8	7.7
Subtotal	123.2	132.3	118.3
Shopping	2.8	3.5	4.9
Educational, religious, civic	2.1	0.7	3.5
Mass media	17.5	10.5	15.4
Social, leisure	11.9	12.6	18.9
Subtotal	34.3	27.3	42.7
Work travel	4.9	3.5	0
Other travel	5.6	4.9	6.3
Total	168.0	168.0	167.3

Source: Hummon (1976).

others because in the daily lives of most Americans, there is relatively little discretion in the amount and scheduling of the time spent in these activities. The next four activities in table 6-4 (that is, shopping; educational, religious, civic; mass media, and social, leisure) are subject to considerably more discretion. In general, these four activities can be viewed as having to fit into the gaps between the nondiscretionary components of an individual's daily time budget.

As indicated in table 6-4, married men and women spend between 71 and 79 percent of their weekly time in relatively nondiscretionary activities. If the amount of time spent in these nondiscretionary activities plus work travel time is netted out of the total weekly time available (that is, 168 hours), the result is the amount of time married adults have available for discretionary activities. For employed married men the figure is 39.9 hours, for employed married women it is 32.2 hours, and for housewives it is 49 hours. Hummon points out that it is within these limited discretionary time budgets that, according to the Nationwide Personal Transportation Study, 63.8 percent of all trips and 53.4 percent of all vehicle miles of travel are made.

It is important to recognize that while time is continuous and infinitely divisible, the use of time is not. As a result, an individual's discretionary time is available in a number of small blocks throughout a week rather than in one continuous block. This results from the daily sequencing of nondiscretionary activities, an important fact that is obscured in time-use studies that simply report aggregate amounts of time spent in different activities.

It would be difficult to disaggregate the weekly aggregate discretionary time budgets reported here into the typical blocks of discretionary time individuals have available. These aggregate discretionary time budgets do, however, indirectly illustrate how the time constraints of different individuals vary. As indicated, employed married women had significantly less discretionary time available in 1965 than their male counterparts and housewives. More specifically, employed married men typically had about 25 percent more weekly discretionary time available than employed married women, and unemployed married women typically had about 50 percent more weekly discretionary time available than employed married women. This observation is especially significant given the rapidly increasing participation of married women in the labor force over the past 30 years.[12]

Data from time-use studies also provide indirect insights into trends in individuals' time constraints. Using 1975 time-use data that are consistent with the 1965 time-use data summarized in table 6-4, Robinson[13] evaluates the differences in how Americans used their time in these two years. Robinson's findings are included in a recent publication on social indicators[14] and are summarized in figure 6-5 and table 6-5. The activities included in this summary are defined as follows:

1. Sleep.
2. Work—includes work breaks.
3. Family care—includes routine and nonroutine housework, shopping, and child care and related travel.
4. Personal care—includes all meals, washing, and dressing.
5. Free time—includes time spent in organizations (class attendance and study, religion, volunteer groups), media (print and broadcast), visiting (at home and away from home), exercise, hobbies, relaxing, entertainment, culture, and all leisure travel.

These activity categories differ from those in table 6–4 and are not conducive to distinguishing between discretionary and nondiscretionary time budgets. Nevertheless, changes in the average weekly amounts of time spent in the preceding five activities from 1965 to 1975 highlight important and insightful trends in time constraints.

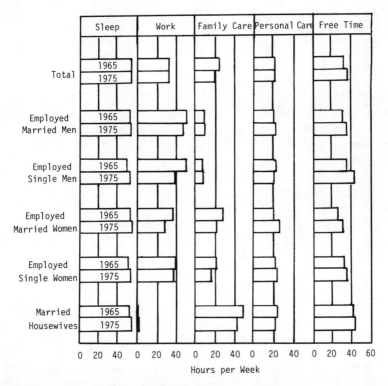

Source: U.S. Department of Commerce (1977).

Figure 6–5. Average Weekly Hours Spent in Major Types of Activities by Selected Population Groups: 1965 and 1975.

Table 6-5
Average Weekly Hours Spent in Major Types of Activities by Selected Population Groups: 1965 and 1975.

Type of Activity	Year	Total Sample	Employed Men		Employed Women		
			Married	Single	Married	Single	Married Housewives
Sleep	1965	53.3	53.1	50.6	53.8	52.6	53.9
	1975	54.7	53.4	54.1	55.1	54.3	56.8
	Difference	1.4	0.3	3.5	1.3	1.7	2.9
	Percent diff.	2.6	0.6	6.9	2.4	3.2	5.4
Work	1965	33.0	51.3	51.4	38.4	39.8	0.5
	1975	32.5	47.4	40.0	30.1	38.8	1.1
	Difference	-0.5	-3.9	-11.4	-8.3	-1.0	0.6
	Percent diff.	-1.5	-7.6	-22.2	-21.6	-2.5	120.0
Family care	1965	25.4	9.0	7.7	28.8	20.6	50.0
	1975	20.5	9.7	9.0	24.9	16.6	44.3
	Difference	-4.9	0.7	1.3	-3.9	-4.0	-5.7
	Percent diff.	-19.3	7.8	16.9	-13.5	-19.4	-11.4
Personal care	1965	21.5	20.9	22.2	20.3	21.7	22.6
	1975	21.8	21.4	20.0	26.2	21.9	21.4
	Difference	0.3	0.5	-2.2	5.9	0.2	-1.2
	Percent diff.	1.4	2.4	-9.9	29.0	0.9	-5.3
Free time	1965	34.8	33.7	36.1	26.7	33.3	41.0
	1975	38.5	36.1	44.9	31.7	36.4	44.4
	Difference	3.7	2.4	8.8	5.0	3.1	3.4
	Percent diff.	10.6	7.1	24.4	18.7	9.3	8.3

Source: U.S. Department of Commerce (1977).

The salient feature of the results presented in figure 6–5 and table 6–5 is that all the groups shown report a greater amount of free time in 1975 than in 1965. From this one is tempted to conclude that, on the average, the control individuals had over the use of their time increased from 1965 to 1975. This conclusion is, however, subject to an important caveat.

Corresponding to the increases in average free time were reductions in the average amounts of time spent working and in family care. The reduction in work hours is in part attributable to trends in the economy. In 1965 the economic boom experienced by the United States associated with the Viet Nam war was at its peak, and the unemployment rate was 4.5 percent. In 1975 the economy was just beginning to recover from the postwar recession, and the unemployment rate was 8.5 percent. This means that for some individuals, the increases in free time recognized in 1975 may have resulted from an involuntary reduction in work hours and therefore an involuntary reduction in income. Thus equating free time with discretionary time when an individual's participation in the work activity is constrained is misleading. Nevertheless, the comparative time–use results presented here suggest that the constraints on activity participation imposed by time availability were not as stringent in 1975 as in 1965. Unfortunately, exactly how these changes manifested themselves in the time constraints of individuals in 1975 cannot be assessed here. One should also recognize that care must be taken when interpreting results based on changes in averages. Such aggregate results obscure the possibility of certain groups of individuals recognizing less control over how they used their time in 1975 than in 1965.

Additional information suggesting that the control individuals have over their time is increasing is found in a *Wall Street Journal* article concerning flexible work schedules.[15] This article indicates that according to a study by the American Management Association, the use of flexible work schedules by U.S. firms has doubled since 1974. Specifically, the study shows that (1) 13 percent of all private employers with fifty workers or more allow employees to vary their daily starting and stopping times while working a contracted number of hours; (2) 6 percent of all employees are on flextime (up to 3.5 million workers); and (3) the trend toward flextime will accelerate. As such, an increasing number of individuals are gaining control over when they start and stop work. Such control does not provide individuals with more discretionary time. Rather, as discussed in chapter 3, it allows individuals to recognize accessibility gains by enhancing their abilities to piece together larger blocks of discretionary time.

While the empirical evidence presented here concerning the time constraints of individuals is fragmentary, this evidence provides important insights into the nature and trends of these constraints. In particular, time-use studies suggest that adults typically have discretion over 20 to 30 percent of their weekly time. Furthermore, these studies indicate that time constraints vary across individuals with different characteristics. In particular, employed married women have more severe constraints on their time than employed married men or housewives.[16] Finally, data on the trends in time use suggest that, on the average, individuals are gaining more control over how they use their time. This increased temporal control suggests that individuals are realizing accessibility gains as a result of shorter work weeks, flexible work schedules, and innovations which are reducing the amounts of time individuals spend maintaining a household.

Assessment of Common Observations Concerning Accessibility

A number of observations are commonly made regarding accessibility. Examples include

1. Accessibility must be on the decline because congestion is increasing.
2. Accessibility must be on the decline because the locations of origins and destinations are becoming more dispersed.
3. Densely developed cities like Paris, San Francisco, and Boston clearly provide more accessibility than sprawling cities like Los Angeles and San Diego.

The following discussion assesses such observations in the context of the data presented in the previous sections and in the context of the present accessibility methodology. This discussion is not directed toward reaching any firm empirical conclusions regarding accessibility. Such an effort exceeds the scope of the surprisingly limited data available on which to base empirical conclusions. Instead, this discussion argues that certain conventional wisdoms regarding accessibility must be viewed with skepticism.

The argument that accessibility is declining because congestion is increasing has evolved from a conception of accessibility that is synonymous with travel times or velocities. However, in light of the conception of accessibility underlying this study, one cannot reach conclusions regarding accessibility trends by looking solely at trends in travel times or velocities. To obtain a more complete picture, changes in the locations of origins and destinations and the time constraints individuals confront must simultaneously be considered. Therefore, even if congestion is increasing, one should not directly conclude that accessibility is decreasing.

The premise that congestion is increasing must also be challenged. While the paucity of hard data relegates the question of actual velocity trends to additional debate, the fragmentary evidence presented here suggests that traffic conditions were significantly better in the late sixties than in previous decades. This is contrary to the commonly held view of transportation analysts that traffic conditions were getting worse over this period.

If automobile speeds have indeed increased, the resulting net accessibility increase depends in part on how urban residents, shopping centers, and firms have adjusted their locations in light of these improvements. Many have speculated that increased automobile speeds stimulate the spatial dispersal of activities (that is, highway improvements generate increased travel and longer travel distances rather than reducing the amount of time allocated to travel). It is concluded based on such speculations that accessibility must be on the decline because locations of origins and destinations are becoming more dispersed. Such a conclusion emerges from conceptualizing accessibility solely in terms of the distances separating activities. As argued throughout this study, the accessibility implications of increases in these distances cannot be assessed only by considering the increases themselves. It is the combined effects of changes in distances and velocities that is important from an accessibility standpoint (given, of course, that time constraints have remained constant).

To illustrate this fact, recall the changes in home-to-work trip lengths and automobile speeds in Detroit and Milwaukee that were alluded to earlier. These changes can be viewed in the context of their *combined effects* on the accessibilities of an *average* commuter residing and working in these areas. It is recognized here that when considering an average individual, the special problems or advantages of individuals in the tails of distributions are neglected. Furthermore, it is recognized that a *change* in mean home-to-work trip lengths is not indicative of the actual distribution of the *change* in home-to-work trip lengths of individuals. Unfortunately, there is not sufficient data to consider these latter issues. Considering only an average commuter does not provide a complete picture of the accessibility balance resulting from increased velocities and increased home-to-work trip lengths, but it does provide important exemplary insights regarding the combined effects of changes in these accessibility-influencing factors.

The increases in average commute speed and home-to-work distance in Detroit from 1953 to 1965 imply that the average automobile commuter in Detroit was spending about 7 percent more time commuting in 1965 than in 1953 (16.2 minutes in 1953 compared with 17.3 minutes in 1965). Moreover, the increases in average commute speed and home-to-work distance in Milwaukee from 1963 to 1972 imply that average automobile commuter in Milwaukee was spending the same amount of time commuting in 1972 as in 1963 (17.9 minutes for both years). These limited observations suggest that the improvements in commute speeds recognized in Detroit and Milwaukee appear to have induced more travel rather than travel-time savings. This is consistent with empirical observations made by Zahavi[17] and with analytical results obtained in case 7 of chapter 5. The changes in home-to-work travel times in Detroit and Milwaukee are not indicative of the net changes in accessibility attributable to the increases in commute speeds and home-to-work distances recognized in both areas. To assess these net impacts, the measure of accessibility developed in case 3 (equation 5.56) is used. This measure is based on the idealized assumptions that activities are homogeneously distributed, the network geometry is a fine grid, and the marginal value of the maximum amount of time available at different locations is constant. Nevertheless, it is applied for exemplary purposes to yield aproximate assessments of the accessibility changes experienced by average commuters in Detroit and Milwaukee.

Figure 6-6 plots BM_3 as a function of an individual's time constraint (τ) for the average commute speeds (v) and home-to-work distances (d) in Detroit in 1953 and 1965. Figure 6-7 provides similar graphs for the average values of v and d in Milwaukee in 1963 and 1972. It is important to recognize that these figures are developed holding all other factors influencing the accessibilities of individuals constant. As such, they reflect the changes in accessibilities resulting only from the changes in automobile commute speed and home-to-work trip length of an average commuter.

As evidenced in figure 6-6, the direction of the net accessibility impact of the increases in average automobile commute speed and average home-to-work distance in Detroit depends on the time constraint of the average commuter. If τ is greater than 0.375 hours (22.5 minutes), the ability of the average commuter to get to locations other than his work location faster than before (as a result of his increased speed) more than compensates for the additional constraint imposed on him by the longer work trip. In addition, for values of τ less than 0.375 hours, there is not enough time available in addition to the required travel time between work and home to allow the increased speed to compensate for the additional constraint imposed by the longer work trip. In Milwaukee (figure 6-7), where the average home-to-work travel time did not change between 1963 and 1972, accessibility gains are recognized for all values of τ.

Observe that as τ increases in both Detroit and Milwaukee, the net accessibility gain increases. This is consistent with the conclusion reached in chapter 5, indicating that the more time an individual has available, the more the individual can take advantage of a velocity increase.

Three conclusions are illustrated in figures 6-6 and 6-7 which challenge conventional wisdoms regarding accessibility. First, changes in accessibility cannot be assessed by examining only changes in velocities *or* changes in the locations of origins and destinations. Instead, from an accessibility standpoint, it is the *combined* effects of velocity changes and dispersion that are important.

Second, depending on an individual's discretionary time budget, it is possible for an individual to spend more time traveling to work (or some

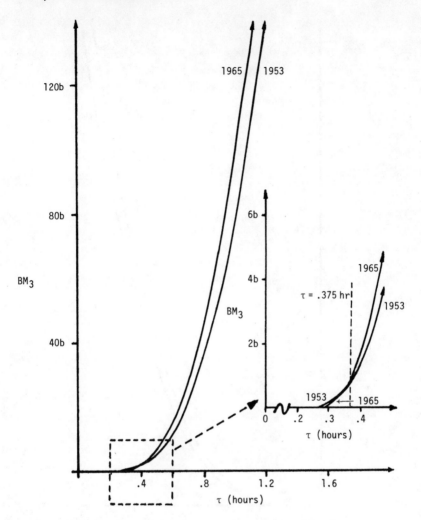

Figure 6-6. BM_3 versus τ for Average Commute Speeds and Home-to-Work Distances in Detroit in 1953 and 1965.

central location like a CBD) and still recognize accessibility gains. More specifically, a velocity increase allows one to move farther from work (both in distance and time) and still reach locations other than work faster. Therefore, dispersion does not necessarily imply a reduction in accessibility. This conclusion is contrary to conclusions often made concerning accessibility that are based on narrowly conceived measures of accessibility like travel time to some central place or distance between activities.

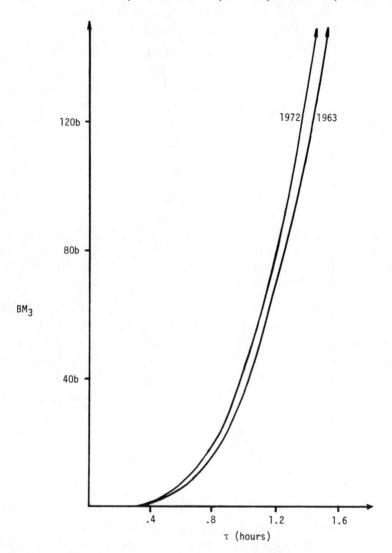

Figure 6–7. BM$_3$ versus τ for Average Commute Speeds and
Home–to–Work Distances in Milwaukee in 1963 and 1972.

Finally, figures 6–6 and 6–7 illustrate the dependence of the accessibility impacts of transportation and spatial changes on the temporal flexibility of individuals. As such, a more complete picture of the impacts of transportation and spatial changes is obtained by considering the temporal dimension of the behavioral spaces of individuals.

The dependence of accessibility on the combined effects of velocities and distances between activities also sheds a different light on comparisons between the accessibility of individuals residing in cities that are quite different in urban form. While densely developed cities have activities which are located closer together than in sprawling cities, they are also typically characterized by average automobile velocities that are lower than those in less-dense cities. For example, in 1970 the population density of Boston was slightly more than twice that of Los Angeles (6,073 versus 13,936 people per square mile). And, as indicated in a study by Fauth, Ingram, and Kroch,[18] the average automobile velocity and trip length in Boston were both slightly over one-half the average automobile velocity and trip length in Los Angeles (19.1 versus 36.5 mi/h and 9.9 versus 19.13 miles, respectively). Consequently, in each region, the average automobile trip took about the same amount of time and circumscribed an area with about the same population. Based on such evidence, it is difficult to judge whether an average Boston resident or Los Angeles resident has more accessibility. This is in contrast to conclusions that are reached using accessibility measures which are essentially synonomous with urban density.

Data Required for a Detailed Empirical Analysis of Accessibility

Automobile travel characteristics and home-to-work distances have been the subjects of much discussion among transportation planners over the past three decades, and time-use studies are becoming popular instruments of social scientists. However, surprisingly little *systematic* data are currently available to empirically address questions concerning accessibility. This results in part from the fact that most past data-collection efforts have been motivated by the self-evident importance of the empirics and not broad paradigms regarding accessibility. As such, these data do not allow a detailed empirical analysis of accessibility as it is conceptualized here.

Ideally, data on the relative locations, sequencing, and durations of the coupling constraints confronted by individuals, the speeds these individuals can travel, and the characteristics of individuals and their households should be sought. Such data could be extracted from detailed weekly diaries of individuals and information on the extent to which they are constrained to participate in different activities. To reflect interdependencies between coupling constraints confronted by members of the same household, diaries could be collected for all members.

Data at this level of detail would serve three important functions. First, they would provide additional insights into the value of the fundamental variables incorporated in the accessibility measures developed here. These insights are important to assess the degree to which individuals are currently constrained and to provide a benchmark for studies of trends in accessibility. Second, they would allow assessment of relationships between characteristics of individuals and households and the accessibility constraints they confront. These relationships are critical for evaluating the effects of changing lifestyles on accessibility. Finally, these data would provide insights into the distributions of individuals with respect to their accessibilities. Such information is essential for identifying groups of significantly constrained and significantly enabled individuals, for assessing the distributional impacts of different strategies, and for purposes of aggregation.

7 Directions for Future Research

This chapter identifies a number of directions for future research pertaining directly to the conceptual framework developed and applied here.[1] These directions are included in four categories:

1. Technical augmentations of the accessibility methodology.
2. Conceptual augmentations of the accessibility methodology.
3. Empirical augmentations of the accessibility methodology.
4. Other applications of the space–time representation of human activity underlying the accessibility methodology.

Brief discussions of the directions comprising each category follow.

Technical Augmentations of the Accessibility Methodology

This category comprises directions for future research that augment the technical development of the accessibility methodology as it is currently conceptualized. Of particular interest and relevance are technical augmentations of

1. The manner in which transportation is represented.
2. The manner in which coupling contraints are represented.
3. The accessibility–measurement framework.

Discussions of each of these follow.

Transportation Augmentation

At this point, the accessibility methodology has been developed with a simplistic view of the abilities of individuals to overcome space. In particular, individuals are assumed to have unfettered access to unscheduled and unrouted transportation that allows travel at a constant maximum velocity over an idealized network at all times of the day. Two important augmentations of this view of transportation concern the scheduling and routing characteristics of various transportation systems and the variability of the velocities individuals can sustain with respect to the time of day and to their location in relation to networks.

While walking, bicycles, and automobiles are unscheduled and unrouted, numerous other modes operate on a timetable, have limited routing, and/or must be accessed at stations. This is illustrated in figure 7-1, which classifies a number of modes with respect to users' perceptions of their routing and scheduling variability. Since routes, schedules, and stations are spatial and temporal characteristics of transportation systems, their accessibility implications can be examined in the context of how they affect space-time prisms. These effects are illustrated simplistically in figures 7-2 and 7-3.

The routing and scheduling characteristics of a public transportation system are depicted in space-time in figure 7-2 (with space in one dimension). In this figure, public transportation lines are represented by parallel trajectories. The constant slopes of these trajectories reflect the maximum average velocity of the public transportation vehicles (that is, the line-haul velocity) and the vertical spacings between them represent the headways between vehicles. These vehicles can only be accessed at stations. The vertical dotted lines in figure 7-2 extrapolate the locations of stations through time. The intersections of these dotted lines and the vehicle trajectories represent the space-time constraints imposed by the public transportation system. Individuals must rendezvous with these intersection points to use the system.

Now consider an individual with an initial origin and a final destination with the same location. Assume that this individual has access to the transportation system depicted in figure 7-2. Also assume that his common origin and destination location is halfway between two stations and that his station-access velocity is (for illustrative purposes) less than the line-haul velocity of the public transportation vehicles. The space-time prism corresponding to the individual's situation is presented in figure 7-3. This prism illustrates the manner in which station spacing, scheduling, line-haul speeds, and access speeds of transportation systems combine to affect the accessibilities of individuals using them. An important direction of future research concerns the development of accessibility measures that incorporate these design parameters. Such measures can be applied to analyze and compare the accessibility implications of a variety of design and operating strategies (for example, tradeoffs between headways and service areas). They can also be applied to compare the accessibility provided by scheduled and routed modes to that provided by personal transportation.

Relaxing the assumption that individuals can sustain a constant maximum velocity over an idealized network at all times of the day is another desirable transportation augmentation. In reality, these maximum velocities vary with the time of day and across networks. This is due to the

Scheduling

	Fixed	Variables
Fixed	Local Bus Express Bus Rapid Rail	Moving Belt
Variable	Subscription Service	Taxi Dial-a-Ride Walking Bicycle Automobile

Routing

Figure 7-1. Users' Perceptions of the Routing and Scheduling Variability of Various Modes.

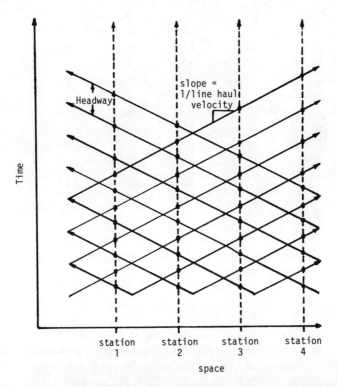

Figure 7-2. Space-Time Representation of the Routing and Scheduling Characteristics of a Public Transportation System.

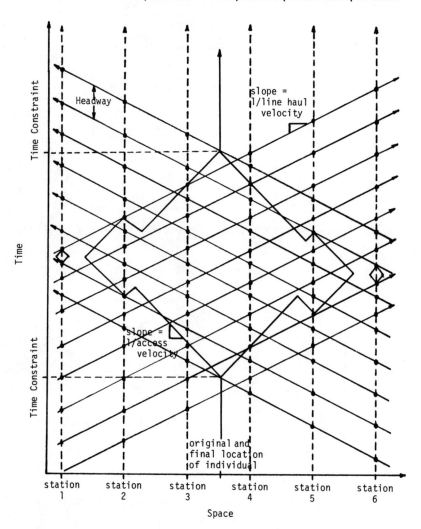

Figure 7-3. Space–Time Prism of an Individual with Access to Public Transportation.

variability of travel demand with the time of day and the variability of the capacities and speed limits of the links that comprise networks. Since these are spatial and temporal variations in velocities, they can be represented in a space–time framework by variations in the slopes of trajectories. (See figures 3-9 and 3-10 for examples of how this can be accomplished.) Accessibility measures can also be developed that reflect this variability. These measures would be applicable in assessing the accessibility implications of strategies that influence capacities on specific links or strategies that control the temporal variability of travel demand.

Augmentations of Coupling Constraints

Coupling constraints are defined in this dissertation as occurring when individuals join other individuals or objects at spatially and temporally fixed locations in order to participate in activities. While all activities have the properties of duration, a position in time (that is, a start time), a place in a sequence of events, and a location or path in space, there are only a very limited set of activities that possess rigid or inflexible coupling constraints. Work and school are common examples. For most other activities there is variation in freedom of choice with regard to whether, where, and when individuals join with other individuals or objects to participate in activities.

A fruitful direction of future research would be the development of a less rigid conceptualization of the constraints individuals confront in space and time. Rather than viewing inflexible coupling constraints as deterministic points in space–time, these constraints could be viewed as being probabilistic. More specifically, distributions could be associated with both the temporal and spatial dimensions of a coupling constraint. Jointly, these distributions would reflect the probability of an individual having to occupy a certain point at a certain time. Specifications of these joint distributions would allow development of *expected* accessibility measures that could be applied to analyze and compare different strategies.

Augmentation of the Accessibility-Measurement Framework

The accessibility-measurement frameworks developed in chapter 4 can be augmented in two ways. First, this framework is based on the assumption that individuals value their abilities to reach locations relative to the *amount* of time they can spend there. Because the availability of activities varies with the time of day, week, or year, individuals value reaching locations relataive to the precise *periods* of time they can occupy them. As such, a more general measurement framework that incorporates the temporal distributions of activities would provide a valuable supplement to the existing methodology.

Second, the existing measurement framework focuses on the accessibility provided by a single space-time prism. In actuality, an individual's existence consists of a sequence of space-time prisms connected by the activity stays associated with coupling constraints. Broadening the accessibility-measurement framework to encompass the opportunities defined by a set of space-time prisms would therefore be a valuable contribution.

Conceptual Augmentations of the Accessibility Methodology

This category comprises directions for future research that augment the conceptual framework developed here. Of particular interest and relevance are conceptual augmentations that

1. Incorporate additional constraints which affect the accessibilities of individuals.
2. Consider household accessibilities as well as the accessibilities of individuals.
3. Consider the dynamics of accessibility change.

Discussions of each of these follow.

Incorporation of Additional Constraints

In the study of accessibility presented here, attention is focused on the transportation, temporal, and spatial constraints which limit the abilities of individuals to participate in activities. These constraints are emphasized because they are affected by a broad variety of accessibility–enhancing strategies at the disposal of transportation planners, urban planners, and decisionmakers. Numerous other constraints exist which are not incorporated in the present conceptualization. Of particular importance are income constraints and sociological constraints. Augmenting the existing conceptualization of the accessibility methodology by incorporating these constraints are important directions for future research.

Since income enables individuals to purchase goods and services, income constraints affect accessibilities in a number of ways. In particular, money is typically required to overcome space and to participate in activities once their location is reached. The more income an individual has, the less of a barrier the monetary costs of travel and the nontravel costs of activity participation become. An individual's income also affects the transportation, temporal, and spatial constraints he confronts. Specifically, income is instrumental in determining the transportation an individual has access to (especially automobiles), his residential location (and therefore the distances he must overcome to participate in different activities), and his ability to purchase services that eliminate or relax time constraints (for example, gardening, day care, or maid services).

It is important to recognize that income constraints are interrelated with temporal and spatial constraints. One must typically invest time to earn an income and improve skills in order to increase wages (through education). Furthermore, one's opportunity for employment can depend on residential location relative to the locations of job opportunities. These interdependencies must not be overlooked in efforts to incorporate income constraints into the present accessibility methodology.

Sociological constraints are those constraints imposed by social problems and the social needs of individuals. Racial and sexual discrimination are examples of sociological constraints. These constraints are related to the spatial and temporal organization of social structures. Individuals are often constrained to partake in activities by the knowledge they have about their environment, peer pressures, and by limiting their behavioral spaces to turf that is defined by their niche in the social structure. While difficult to conceptualize in an analytical framework, the behavioral constraints imposed by social structure and the effects of social structure on urban morphology should not be neglected. These constraints may very well lie at the root of the accessibility problem confronted by different classes of individuals.

Household Accessibilities

The unit of analysis throughout this study of accessibility has been the individual. While it is indeed individuals who have accessibility, studies of their accessibilities are incomplete without considering their roles as household members.

Clearly, the accessibility of an individual in a household of other individuals depends not only on his own characteristics, but also on the characteristics of the household itself. Household residential location and automobile ownership decisions, the employment decisions of different household members, household income, and household size and stage in life cycle both enhance and constrain the accessibilities of all members.

An understanding of the interdependencies of household members is needed to examine the accessibilities of special groups of individuals (for example, housewives and children) and for assessing the accessibility implications of trends in family structure, the participation of women in the labor force, and life cycle. As such, augmenting the existing conceptualization of accessibility by considering individuals as household members is an important direction for future research.

Dynamics of Accessibility Change

The accessibility methodology developed here captures the interdependencies of a number of factors that influence accessibility. It is applied to assess the direct accessibility consequences of changes in these factors.

This short-run descriptive analysis of accessibility change does not attempt to assess the longer-run dynamics of accessibility change. These long-run dynamics are clearly quite complex. However, if questions concerning the combined short- and long-run accessibility implications of the interdependent trends in congestion, housing prices, income, fuel prices, automobile prices, and lifestyles are to be addressed, an understanding of the dynamics of accessibility change is mandatory. Gaining such understanding is an important area of future research.

Empirical Augmentations of the Accessibility Methodology

Chapter 6 supplements the methodological study of accessibility presented in this book by providing some empirical insights concerning accessibility. Emerging from this chapter is the recognition that surprisingly little systematic data are available to empirically address questions concerning trends in accessibility and questions concerning the distribution of the population with respect to accessibility. As such, a critical direction for future research concerns data-collection efforts. A discussion of the nature of the data required for an indepth empirical analysis of accessibility as it is conceived of here, how these data could be collected, and the questions to which they would be applied is provided in chapter 6.

Other Applications of the Space-Time Representation
of Human Activity Underlying the Accessibility Methodology

As discussed by Pred,[2] Hägerstrand's space-time representation of human activity has a number of possible applications. Besides its applicability in accessibility modeling, two additional applications are of particular interest here.

The first involves using Hägerstrand's representation as a guide to specifying models of the transportation-related behavior of individuals. Since the pioneering work of Warner,[3] urban transportation research has placed priorities on understanding the underlying determinants of trip-making behavior. To gain such understanding, researchers have concentrated on developing models of the short-run travel decisions of individuals faced with a given set of travel opportunities.[4] A major criticism of these models is that they are in general poorly specified. This is due in part to the neglect in most specifications of factors that determine the opportunities available to individuals. Such neglect is a critical oversight because, in many circumstances, trip-making behavior depends a great deal on factors constraining the abilities of individuals to make trips. Since Hägerstrand's framework allows one to systematically view a number of factors that constrain trip making, it has the potential of providing valuable insights into more appropriate specifications of models of trip–making behavior.

The second application of Hägerstrand's representation involves its use in rethinking the value of time theories developed by economists and the applications of such theories in studies of transportation.[5]

In contrast to the economic value of time theories, Hägerstrand's representation forces one to view time in a nonmonetary context. Specifically, this representation suggests that individuals value their time relative to the alternative uses of time that are available to them. These alternative uses have spatial components; they vary with the time of day, week, or year; and they are rooted in the past experiences of individuals. Indirect monetary values of time do not reflect these subtleties. Therefore, it is important to begin viewing time allocation directly in real terms (that is, substantive terms) rather than indirectly in monetary terms.

Notes

Chapter 1
Introduction

1. See Hoggart (1973) for a comprehensive bibliography on the concept of accessibility.
2. Chapin (1974).
3. Owen (1972).
4. Chapin (1974).
5. Foley (1975).
6. Hägerstrand (1970, 1974).
7. These are the rationales on which Hägerstrand's writings (1970, 1974) are in part based.
8. Hägerstrand (1970, 1974, 1975).
9. As discussed in Jones (1978), this winding down was fueled by a combination of (1) the transportation cost-revenue squeeze, (2) political opposition, initially, to highway construction and, now, to rapid transit construction, and (3) a crumbling of the alliance of fiscal stabilization and economic growth and revitalization that drove the transportation capital investment machinery.
10. Hägerstrand (1970).
11. See Weibull (1976) for a discussion of the characteristics of existing accessibility measures.

Chapter 2
Hägerstrand's Space-Time Representation of Human Activity

1. Hägerstrand (1970, 1974, 1975).
2. To date, the bulk of the time geography literature is in Swedish. Fortunately, Pred (1973) provides an extensive paraphrased English summary of the fundamental ideas and components of Hägerstrand's model, and Pred (1977) discusses the intents and planning applications of time-geography and other possible uses of this framework. For this reason, only those aspects of time-geography which directly concern this study are expanded upon here.
3. Hägerstrand (1970).
4. Pred (1973, 1977).
5. Hägerstrand (1975).

Chapter 3
The Space–Time Implications of Transportation, Temporal, and Spatial Strategies

1. Hummon (1976).
2. Lenntorp (1976).
3. Ibid.
4. For a discussion of idealized network geometries, see Newell (1977).

Chapter 4
Benefits of Space–Time Autonomy

1. This discussion emerged from conversations with Professor Martin Wachs, School of Architecture and Urban Planning, University of California, Los Angeles.
2. For a discussion of the concept of "option" value, see Krutilla and Fisher (1975).
3. Weibull (1976).
4. Smith (1975).
5. Weibull (1976).

Chapter 5
Analytical Comparisons of Different Strategies

1. Wachs and Kumagai (1973).
2. Lenntorp (1976).
3. Weibull (1976).
4. Wilson (1970).
5. For a detailed discussion of economic utility theory, see Lancaster (1971). For examples of applications of utility theory concepts to problems in transportation, see Golob and Beckmann (1971); Beckmann and Golob (1972); Golob, Gustafson, and Beckmann (1973); Beckmann, Gustafson, and Golob (1973); and Beckmann and Golob (1974).
6. For a discussion of applications of the power–function specification to problems in transportation, see Golob and Beckmann (1971).
7. These empirical observations are documented by Zahavi (1974, 1978).
8. For a discussion of these specifications, see Golob and Beckmann (1971) and Beckmann, Gustafson, and Golob (1973).

9. Wilson (1970).
10. Beckmann and Golob (1972).
11. *Wall Street Journal*, April 11, 1978.
12. For a historical discussion of the political economy of urban high-way investments, see Jones (1978).
13. Data for figure 5-23 were obtained from U.S. Department of Commerce (1978).
14. A national conference on alternative work schedules was held in Chicago on March 21-22, 1977.

Chapter 6
Empirical Considerations

1. Koltnow (1970).
2. U.S. Department of Transportation (1973).
3. Koltnow (1970).
4. U.S. Department of Transportation (1973).
5. For a detailed discussion of these factors, see Bellomo, Dial, and Voorhees (1970) and U.S. Department of Transportation (1973).
6. Bellomo, Dial, and Voorhees (1970).
7. Southeastern Wisconsin Regional Planning Commission (1975).
8. For a summary of time-use and time-allocation studies, see Chapin (1974) and Robinson (1977).
9. Becker (1965).
10. This study was part of a multinational time-use study encompassing twelve nations (Szalai, 1972). Robinson (1977) includes analysis regarding the time use of Americans based on this 1965 data.
11. Hummon (1976).
12. According to Keyserling (1976), as of March 1975 the percent of working mothers with children aged 6 to 17 has doubled since 1948 (up to 55 percent) and the percent of working mothers with children less than 6 years old has tripled from 13 percent in 1948 to 39 percent in 1975. For a time-geographic perspective of the constraints confronted by women, see Palm and Pred (1974).
13. Robinson (1976).
14. U.S. Department of Commerce (1977).
15. *Wall Street Journal*, April 11, 1978.
16. These constraints are referred to by Palm and Pred (1974) as role-ascribed constraints.
17. Zahavi (1974, 1978).
18. Fauth, Ingram, and Kroch (1975).

Chapter 7
Directions for Future Research

1. For a broad discussion of future avenues of inquire regarding the unification of spatially and temporally structured studies of society, see Part VI in Carlstein, Parkes, and Thrift (1978).

2. Pred (1977).

3. Warner (1962).

4. For a detailed discussion of these models, see Domencich and McFadden (1975).

5. See Becker (1965), Linder (1970), and Ghez and Becker (1975); for a critique of these theories, see Carlstein, Parkes, and Thrift (1978).

Bibliography

Barton-Aschman Associates, American Institute of Planners, and Motor Vehicle Manufacturers Association. 1974. *Urban Transportation Factbook,* Part 1, Table 1-12.

Becker, Gary S. 1965. "A Theory of the Allocation of Time," *The Economic Journal,* pp. 493-517.

Beckmann, M.J., and T.F. Golob. 1972. "On the Metaphysical Foundations of Traffic Flow Theory: Entrophy Revisited." In G.F. Newell, ed., *Traffic Flow and Transportation.* New York: American Elsevier, pp. 109-118.

Beckmann, M.J., R.L. Gustafson, and T.F. Golob. 1973. "Locational Factors in Automobile Ownership Decisions," *Annals of Regional Science* 7, pp. 1-12.

Beckmann, M.J., and T.F. Golob. 1974. "Traveler Decisions and Traffic Flows: A Behavioral Theory of Network Equilibrium," in D.V. Buckley, ed., *Transportation and Traffic Flow.* Sydney: Reed, pp. 453-482.

Bellomo, S.J., R.B. Dial, and A.M. Voorhees. 1970. *Factors, Trends, and Guidelines Related to Trip Length.* National Cooperative Highway Research Program Report 89, Highway Research Board.

Carlstein, T., D. Parkes, and N. Thrift. 1978. "Now Where do the Arrows Go?" Part VI of *Timing Space and Spacing Time in Socio-Economic Systems.* London: Edward Arnold (forthcoming).

Chapin, Stuart F. 1974. *Human Activity Patterns in the City.* New York: Wiley.

Domencich, T.A., and D. McFadden. 1975. *Urban Travel Demand: A Behavioral Analysis.* New York: American Elsevier.

Fauth, G.R., G.K. Ingram, and E. Kroch. 1975. "Cost Effectiveness of Emission Reduction and Transportation Control Policies," *International Journal of Transport Economics* 2, no. 1, Table 1.

Foley, Donald L. 1975. "Accessibility for Residents in the Metropolitan Environment." In Amos H. Hawley and Vincent P. Rock, eds., *Metropolitan America and Contemporary Perspective.* New York: Sage, pp. 157-198.

———. 1977. *Improving Accessibility for the Carless.* Institute of Transportation Studies, University of California, Berkeley.

Ghez, G.R., and G.S. Becker. 1975. *The Allocation of Time Over the Life Cycle.* New York: Columbia Univ. Press.

Golob, T.F., and M.J. Beckmann. 1971. "A Utility Model for Travel Forecasting," *Transportation Science,* 5, no. 1.

Golob, T.F., R.L. Gustafson, and M.J. Beckmann. 1973. "An Economic Utility Theory Approach to Spatial Interaction," *Papers of the Regional Science Association* 30, pp. 159–182.

Hägerstrand, T. 1970. "What about People in Regional Science?" *Papers of the Regional Science Association* 24, pp. 7–21.

——— 1974. "The Impact of Transport on the Quality of Life," topic 5 in *Transport in the 1980-1990 Decade*. European Conference of Ministeres of Transport, 5th Symposium, Athens, Greece.

——— 1975. "Space, Time and the Human Condition." In A. Karlquist, L. Lundquist, and F. Snickars, eds., *Dynamic Allocation of Urban Space*. Lexington, Mass: Saxon House, Lexington Books, D.C. Heath.

Hoggart, K. 1973. *Transportation Accessibility: Some References Concerning Applications, Definitions, Importance and Index Construction*. Council of Planning Librarians Exchange Bibliography 482.

Hummon, N. 1976. *Analysis of Four Institutional Settings and the Role of the Automobile*. Task 4 Report, University of Pittsburgh, DOT Contract DOT-OS-50242.

Jones, David W. 1978. "Urban Highway Investment and Political Economy of Fiscal Retrenchment." In Alan Altshuler, ed., *Current Issues in Transportation Policy*. Lexington, Mass.: Lexington Books, D.C. Heath.

Keyserling, Mary Dublin. 1976. "The Economic Status of Women in the United States," *American Economic Review Papers and Proceedings* 66, no. 2, pp. 205–212.

Koltnow, Peter. 1970. *Changes in Mobility in American Cities*. Highway Users Federation for Safety and Mobility, Washington, D.C.

Krutilla, J.F., and A.C. Fisher. 1975. *The Economics of Natural Environment: Studies in the Valuation of Commodity and Amenity Resources*. Baltimore: John Hopkins Univ. Press.

Lancaster, K. 1971. *Consumer Demand: A New Approach*. New York: Columbia Univ. Press.

Lenntorp, B. 1976. "Paths in Space–Time Environments: A Time Geography Study of Movement Possibilities of Individuals," *Lund Studies in Geography No. 44*. The Royal University of Lund, Sweden.

Linder, Staffan. 1970. *The Harried Leisure Class*. New York: Columbia Univ. Press.

Newell, Gordon. 1977. "Traffic Flow on Transportation Networks." Unpublished Lecture Notes, Department of Civil Engineering, University of California, Berkeley.

Owen, Wilfred. 1972. *The Accessible City*. Washington: Brookings Institute.

Palm, R., and A. Pred. 1974. *A Time Geographic Perspective on Problems of Inequality for Women*. Working Paper 236, Institute of Urban and Regional Development, University of California, Berkeley.

Pred, Allan. 1973. "Urbanization, Domestic Planning Problems and Swedish Geographic Research," *Progress in Geography* 5, pp. 1–76.

———. 1977. "The Choreography of Existence: Comments on Häger-strand's Time–Geography and Its Usefulness," *Economic Geography* 53, no. 2.

Robinson, John P. 1976. "Changes in American's Use of Time, 1965–1975," *Report of the Communication Research Center.* Cleveland State University.

——— 1977. *How Americans Use Time: A Social Psychological Analysis of Everyday Behavior.* New York: Praeger.

Southeastern Wisconsin Regional Planning Commission. 1975. "A Regional Land Use Plan and a Regional Transportation Plan for Southeastern Wisconsin—2000," *Planning Report* 25.

Smith, T. 1975. "A Choice Theory of Spatial Interaction," *Regional Science and Urban Economics* 5, no. 2.

Szalia, Alexander, ed. 1972. *The Use of Time.* The Hague: Mouton.

United States Department of Commerce. 1977. *Social Indicators 1976.* Office of the Federal Statistical Policy and Standards, Bureau of the Census.

U.S. Department of Commerce. 1978. *Statistical Abstract of the United States.* Bureau of the Census. 99th ed.

United States Department of Transportation. 1973. *National Personal Transportation Study,* Report No. 8, "Home–to–Work Trips and Travel."

Wachs, M., and T.G. Kumagai: 1973. "Physical Accessibility as a Social Indicator," *Socio-Economic Planning Sciences* 7, pp. 437–456.

Wall Street Journal, 1978. "A Special News Report on People and Their Jobs in Offices, Fields, and Factories," April 11, 1978.

Warner, S.L. 1962. *Stochastic Choice Model in Urban Travel: A Study in Binary Choice.* Evanston, Ill.: Northwestern Univ. Press.

Weibull, J. 1976. "An Axiomatic Approach to the Measurement of Accessibility," *Regional Science and Urban Economics* 6, pp. 356–379.

Wilson, A.G. 1970. *Entropy in Urban and Regional Modeling.* London: Pion.

Zahavi, Y. 1974. *Travel Time Budgets and Mobility in Urban Areas.* Federal Highway Administration, U.S. Department of Transportation, Report FHWA–PL–8183.

. 1978. "Measurement of Travel Demand and Mobility." Paper Presented at the Joint International Meeting on the Integration of Traffic and Transportation Engineering in Urban Areas, Tel Aviv, Israel, December 17–22.

Index

About the Author

Lawrence D. Burns is an associate senior research engineer in the Transportation and Traffic Science Department of the General Motors Research Laboratories. He was educated at General Motors Institute (B.S. Mechanical Engineering, 1975), the University of Michigan (M.S. Public Systems Engineering, 1975), and the University of California, Berkeley (Ph.D. Civil Engineering, 1978). Dr. Burns has published in a variety of transportation-related journals and is a member of the Editorial Advisory Board of the journal *Transportation Research*. In addition to the subject of this book, Dr. Burns' research interests include transportation economics, freight transportation, and the future of automobile transportation.